TWAYNE'S WORLD AUTHORS SERIES

A Survey of the World's Literature

Sylvia E. Bowman, Indiana University

GENERAL EDITOR

NEW ZEALAND

Joseph Jones, University of Texas

EDITOR

John Mulgan

(*TWAS 58*)

TWAYNE'S WORLD AUTHORS SERIES (TWAS)

The purpose of TWAS is to survey the major writers —novelists, dramatists, historians, poets, philosophers, and critics—of the nations of the world. Among the national literatures covered are those of Australia, Canada, China, Eastern Europe, France, Germany, Greece, India, Italy, Japan, Latin America, New Zealand, Poland, Russia, Scandinavia, Spain, and the African nations, as well as Hebrew, Yiddish, and Latin Classical literatures. This survey is complemented by Twayne's United States Authors Series and English Authors Series

The intent of each volume in these series is to present a critical-analytical study of the works of the writer; to include biographical and historical material that may be necessary for understanding, appreciation, and critical appraisal of the writer; and to present all material in clear, concise English—but not to vitiate the scholarly content of the work by doing so.

John Mulgan

By P. W. DAY

University of Manitoba

Twayne Publishers, Inc. :: New York

Preface

IT will perhaps be asked why it was thought necessary to publish a biographical and critical study of an author whose creative work is as slender in output as the bibliography at the end of
this book reveals. The question deserves an answer.

John Mulgan was a man of letters in the widest sense of the
term. As a member of the secretariat of the Clarendon Press, he
had dealings with literary and academic people in many different
places (one of his first assignments was to set about the planning
of what ultimately became the *Oxford History of English Literature*). As a part-time journalist, he showed his skill at registering
impressions and transmitting them in lucid vigorous prose.

The prose of his newspaper articles reveals something of his
individual nature—something of the intelligence and charm to
which all who knew him bear witness. But these qualities, though
admirable, would hardly qualify their possessor for the serious
treatment which a study such as this implies.

It is in the newspaper articles, however, that a trace may be
found of a reason for considering Mulgan seriously. The series of
newsletters on current events which Mulgan wrote (along with G.
S. Cox) for a special column in the *Auckland Star* in the year
1936–37 reveals one specific fact—that he had a highly developed
social conscience. He really cared that people in general should be
well-informed on public events; and he cared because he was conscious of the deficiencies of the so-called democracies.

Such a feeling should not be dismissed as typical young man's
misty Marxism of the 1930's. As the facts of his life will show,
Mulgan displayed, at every turn of his career, an awareness of the
hard realities that constitute a political system. He was not an
optimist. But he believed that it was not beyond the wit of man to
ameliorate social conditions and improve the lot of the average
citizen. How this might be done was his constant preoccupation.

In the context of New Zealand letters, Mulgan is a member of the generation which contained those poets who first spoke with the accent of New Zealand, not, as previous generations had done, with the borrowed accent of the Mother Country. He is a contemporary of Denis Glover, who in the voice of Harry, the "casual man," recounts an experience wholly antipodean.

What shall we sing? sings Harry.

Sing all things sweet or harsh upon
These islands in the Pacific sun,
The mountains whitened endlessly
And the white horses of the winter sea
    sings Harry.

That generation—Glover, Fairburn, Brasch, Curnow, Mason, are the poets concerned—showed an awareness of their land and its qualities which was new and vital. No prose writer of similar power seemed to be in existence. Yet a study of Mulgan reveals his fitness to stand with the poets just named. This is on the strength of a single novel and a roughly sketched book of memoirs.

The plain fact is that *Man Alone,* published as war burst on Europe and forgotten until ten years later, has become established as the first serious achievement in the novel form by a New Zealand writer. In it Mulgan reveals an awareness of and a sensitivity to New Zealand and its values which is no less than that shown by his poet contemporaries. In its way, it goes far beyond anything written up to that time in subtlety and power.

These qualities also mark *Report on Experience,* composed in Cairo and Athens when the war was nearing its climax. This book, even more than *Man Alone,* marks its author off as an idealist with a powerful sense of reality. These mature reflections of a New Zealander wise beyond his years continue the quest of the thirties for a more equitable social structure. The lessons of the war are interpreted with unemphatic but pungent common sense, and with an undercurrent of humane feeling to which Mulgan's contact with the Greeks had given special force. For he sees the lives of the poor everywhere as composed of simple things of which they are all too easily robbed by society's specific organizations. His view resembles Bernard Spencer's in his poem "Greek Excavations":

> The minimum wish
> For the permanence of the basic things of a life,
> For children and friends and having enough to eat,
> And the great key of skill;
> The life the generals and bankers cheat.

Considering these facts, it is not extravagant to see Mulgan, in spite of his slender output, as a significant figure in the literature of New Zealand.

In the biographical section of this study, most attention has been given to two periods of Mulgan's life: his life at Oxford, and his year in the Greek mountains as a guerrilla fighter. In the detail of the latter period may be seen something of the intolerable strain which undoubtedly contributed to the breakdown that resulted in Mulgan's taking his own life.

University of Manitoba   P. W. DAY

Acknowledgments

Acknowledgments are due to many people who have been good enough to help me in various ways; in particular to Mr. R. G. Mulgan (for permission to use his father's letters); Lady Turner; Dr. K. Sisam; Mr. A. L. P. Norrington, President of Trinity College, Oxford; Mr. D. M. Davin (for permission to quote from his article in *Landfall*); Sir Geoffrey Cox; Professor J. M. Bertram; Mr. Colin Reeve; Professor Nicholas Hammond; Mr. Michael Ward; Mr. A. Edmonds; Mr. Alfred Borgmann; Mr. L. Northover; Colonel Patrick Wingate; Count Julian Dobrski; Mr. Henry Moazzo (for his great kindness in taking me to the Pindus Mountains); Mrs. Z. Tsiminaki; Mr. E. H. Blow; Mr. E. J. Paterson; Mr. Paul Contomichalos; Miss Sarah Campion; Hon. C. M. Woodhouse; Colonel Boxshall of the War Office; Prof. R. P. Anschutz; Mrs. B. Schiessel; Mr. D. P. Edwards of Bristol University (for the maps).

For permission to quote, thanks are due to: *Landfall;* Pegasus Press and Denis Glover (for permission to quote "The Magpies"); Dr. Allen Curnow (for permission to quote from "The Unhistoric Story").

Contents

Chronology

1911   December 31, born at Christchurch, New Zealand, son of Alan and Marguerita Mulgan.

1916   Alan Mulgan appointed Literary Editor of the *Auckland Star;* family moved to Auckland.

1917   Began primary schooling at Maungawhau School.

1925   Became a boarder at Wellington College.

1927   Went into the Fifth Form at Auckland Grammar School.

1930   Began to read for B.A. degree at Auckland University College.

1931   Nominated for Rhodes Scholarship.

1932   April 14, Auckland Riots began. December, completed B.A. degree. Vice-President of Students' Association. Chairman of Publications Committee.

1933   Freedom of speech controversy. October 8, sailed for England in "Ruahine." November 17, entered Merton College, Oxford.

1935   July, placed in First Class in English Language and Literature. Entered employ of Clarendon Press, Oxford.

1936   Began newsletters to *Auckland Star* (with G. S. Cox).

1937   April, became engaged to Gabrielle Wanklyn. July, marriage to Gabrielle Wanklyn. August, began editing *Poems of Freedom*. December, began *Man Alone*.

1938   January, completed *Poems of Freedom*. May, completed *Man Alone*. December, *Poems of Freedom* published.

1939   March, *Man Alone* accepted by Selwyn and Blount. October, *Man Alone* published. September 3, joined 5th Battalion Oxford and Bucks. as subaltern; adjutant in October.

1940   March 5, Richard Mulgan born. June 28, Gabrielle sailed for Canada on "Duchess of Richmond." June, battalion posted to Northern Ireland.

1941   Promoted Major. Gabrielle sailed to New Zealand (April).

1942 Posted to an infantry regiment as second-in-command; June, sailed for Middle East. August, in action, Western Desert. December, unit detached from 8th Army and sent to 10th Army in Iraq.

1943 May, resigned from unit and joined Force 133. September 12, parachuted into Greece. December, appointed to command Area 3, North Roumeli.

1944 April, sabotage began and continued regularly from then on. June, action at Kaitsa. Americans joined forces in Area 3. July, British troops from R.S.R. arrived. August, Germans ravaged Sperkheios Valley. September, "Operation Noah's Ark" put into effect. October, Germans departed. Went to Cairo. Began *Report on Experience.*

1945 January 14, returned to Athens as Commander Adv. Force 133. April 19, flew to Cairo to report completion of task in Athens. April 25, committed suicide by overdose of morphia.

CHAPTER 1

"Islands in the Pacific Sun"

THE two islands of New Zealand lie on the far rim of the Pacific Ocean. To the traveler by air or sea they are initially a bank of mist on the horizon—the "long white cloud" of the first Maori voyagers, with whom their history begins. In spite of Tasman's brief visit in 1642 it was not until the eighteenth century that the country entered the consciousness of Europe, with the rediscovery of the islands by Captain Cook. From then on it was exploited by Europeans, at first sporadically for the kauri spars from its forests and the whales from its surrounding seas; then systematically, by shiploads of colonists from Great Britain.

Through their efforts, the land passed rapidly from virgin forest to farmland and township. Wars against the Maori inhabitants in the 1860's only sealed the European supremacy. For the remainder of the century the business of civilizing the country went remorselessly on—the business of burning off forest and planting grass in the ashes, of building houses and fencing in livestock, and of sending primary products to the markets of Great Britain.

For it was upon these markets that the infant colony depended. New Zealand's temperate climate gave its farmers the advantage of being able to graze their animals in the open all the year round. In addition to this, a steady rainfall gave constant grass growth, so that few special crops needed to be grown to feed the animal population, which quickly outstripped the human (today animals outnumber humans in the ratio of twenty to one). Hence the cheapness of the butter, cheese, meat, and wool which New Zealand exported to England all through the last half of the nineteenth century—a cheapness which admirably suited the cheap food policy of successive British governments, committed to the expansion of industry.

Such a policy continued up to the outbreak of the First World War, after which cheap and plentiful food became doubly important both to New Zealand and to Great Britain. Prices rose, farming became more profitable than it had ever been; and the tempo of land development quickened still further when the soldiers returning from the war were settled on farms and began, in their turn, to contribute to the productivity of the country.

This war, indeed, and the influenza epidemic which succeeded it, provided New Zealanders with their first experience of large-scale crisis; the results were twofold. First, the myth was born of the dutiful child turning to assist the motherland in time of peril. Though bridling at the name of "colony" (dominion status had been granted in 1907), most New Zealanders felt that the only certainty in foreign affairs lay in the assumption that Britain was always right.

Strangely contradicting this assumption (since it was, if not derived from, at least confirmed by, the experience of the soldiers abroad) was the myth of the island paradise—"God's own Country." Though obviously of exceedingly ancient origin, this myth showed itself in the aggressive assertion of New Zealand superiority (insofar as standards of living and political freedom were concerned) to all other countries in the world.

So it was that the dominion entered the twenties—confident of Great Britain's destiny as head of the Commonwealth and of her own destiny as not the least of the members of that Commonwealth.

This imperialistic euphoria had its effect on the writers of New Zealand. The assumption that England was destined to lead, insensibly caused writers to seek in their own country parallels with English life. Novels and poems on English models were plentiful. Just as the earliest painters had rendered the harsh mountain shapes of New Zealand, and its somber native bush, in terms of the rounded hills of England, and the subdued light and color of the Highlands, so writers seeking to express the quality of life in their own country did so in terms of the traditional plot structures and the traditional social institutions of England. New Zealand life was deemed too unfamiliarly coarse and vulgar to appear in literature undisguised.

For this tendency there was probably a quite deep-seated reason. Settlers convinced themselves and one another that they had triumphed in their conquest of New Zealand. The comparison with England revealed many areas in which the younger country appeared superior—the general standard of housing and the condition of the workers, for instance. By ignoring aspects of life in which New Zealand was clearly backward, or at least, by vaguely expecting that "progress" would make these disappear, it was possible to forget—temporarily—the bleak picture of the interior of the North Island of that time: range upon range of sullen hills, desolate miles of blackened fallen tree trunks, mean farmhouses joined to sickly settlements by clay roads, a single line of narrow gauge railway running precariously from Auckland to Wellington through weary vistas of scrub, gorse, and—here and there—grass.

Small wonder that urban dwellers did their best to blot that picture from their memories, by fixing their eyes on the tram-cars, the fashionable shops, the cinemas, and the street lamps of Auckland, Wellington, Christchurch, and Dunedin.

It was into this world that John Alan Edward Mulgan was born and in it he grew up. When he went abroad, to study and to live in England, he carried with him the sense of life as it was lived in New Zealand, and it is his distinction that he wrote a fine and bitter novel which is, it can be argued, the very first New Zealand novel (with the possible exception of Jane Mander's *Story of a New Zealand River*) to face the unpleasant facts which were there for all to see, and to give them imaginative life.

Later, exhausted and troubled in spirit by campaigning in the mountains of occupied Greece, and recalling his youth, Mulgan was to write a sad but sane and gentle volume of reminiscences, which contains perhaps the most lyrical, pregnant, and condensed account of the nature of New Zealand to be found outside the work of New Zealand poets.

But Mulgan deserves writing about for another reason besides his literary achievement. The short life of this brilliant young man further documents the thought of the 1930's in two principal respects. His life is from one point of view that of a provincial who, exiled in the metropolis, judges his province in retrospect by metropolitan standards. It is from another that of a left-wing intellectual acutely sensitive to and desperately interested in the mechanisms of social change, yet too intelligent and too farsighted to commit himself to the Communist—or any other—party. His attitude is one of analytical yet passionate detachment; it can be documented in the newsletters he sent back to the *Auckland Star*, which reveal a mind wise and mature beyond its years.

Like Yeats's Major Robert Gregory, the appellation "Soldier, Scholar, Horseman . . ." fitted him exactly; and so did the implications of many-sided sympathies and many-faceted talents which Yeats attributes to Gregory. Mulgan, like Gregory, was a distinguished human being.

CHAPTER 2

Auckland and Oxford

MOST people are influenced in their attitude to life by their parents, but John Mulgan was perhaps more directly acted upon than most people: by his mother in a positive, by his father in a negative way.

His mother—born Marguerita Pickmere—was a granddaughter of the missionary Richard Matthews who had landed at the Bay of Islands from H.M.S. "Beagle" in 1835. She was one of the first women in New Zealand to gain an honors degree, taking a first in Latin and English at Auckland University College in 1902. She retained for the whole of her long life (she died in 1965) a keen interest in politics and social questions, and she passed this on to her elder son.

John Mulgan's father—Alan—was very much a public figure. Becoming literary editor of the *Auckland Star* in 1916 (nine years after his marriage in Christchurch to Marguerita Pickmere) he quickly made his mark as a successful journalist and as the author of charming verse in a conventional but unforced Georgian vein. Against his father's literary ideals, however, John Mulgan was destined to rebel quite strongly.

Alan and Marguerita Mulgan's second child, born in Christchurch on January 31, 1911, was christened John Alan Edward. He was barely five years old when the family moved to Auckland, where they settled in Mt. Eden at 12 Landscape Road.

Mulgan's primary school was the suburban one of Maungawhau where the headmaster, "Curly" Olsen gave many young Aucklanders a good academic start in life. In 1926 Mulgan's parents went on a trip to Great Britain for a year (taking their daughter, Dorothea, with them) and put their elder son to board at Wellington College for a year and a term. Then he transferred to the Auckland Grammar School, where he remained until the end of 1929.

Some years after Mulgan's death was reported his third form teacher at Wellington College—A. E. Caddick—wrote a two page memoir to his former pupil, which bore glowing testimony to the latter's liveliness of mind and nascent literary sense.[1]

As a senior pupil at Auckland Grammar School, Mulgan was also praised. The football coach wrote to his father: "It is the Head's expressed opinion that (John) is the best all-rounder that has passed through the school."[2] As well as making an excellent impression in his class work, Mulgan played a good game of rugby football, was a very fair cricketer and boxer, and had from his earliest years been accustomed to sailing small boats on the Manukau and Waitemata Harbours.

In spite of the fine impression he made as a scholar, he did not succeed in gaining a university scholarship in 1929. He was, in fact, several places away from the university scholars, at the upper end of the credit list. Nevertheless, the sound reputation he had made at the grammar school accompanied him to Auckland University College, when he enrolled there for the B.A. course in English and Greek in 1930.

I   The Shadow of Violence

Only a year or two previously the college had moved into the white stone building with the pinnacled Gothic clock tower which Auckland citizens christened "The Wedding Cake." At that stage there were about seven hundred undergraduates—the greater number part-time. Later, in England, Mulgan remembered what it had been like to study as a full-time student in New Zealand:

When we were students in New Zealand, we were very apologetic about it. If we were not at lectures, which being of a low standard we were compelled to attend, we felt that we could only justify ourselves by a continuous application to books, and even in that we blushed before the money-making merchants of the city, when they cared to notice us. But we were saved by having to do this for only six months of the year, and for the rest we could sometimes make the pretence of earning our living. Most of our fellow-students worked all the time in offices, and came in the evenings to our lectures.[3]

One of Mulgan's best friends at this period of his life, Mr. E. J. Paterson of Auckland, vividly remembers a working holiday which he and Mulgan took in the long vacation of 1930–31. They traveled down to Nelson in the South Island, and took a succession of seasonal jobs—pea-picking, fruit-picking, tobacco hoeing, and general farm work. Then for the last fortnight they took their bedrolls and tramped from Ngatimoti over the top of Mt. Arthur, then in a wide arc across the wild country to Takaka.

Mulgan was, without a doubt, a popular and energetic figure in student affairs. As well as standing out as a footballer and a boxer, he became a prominent member of the student executive, and was in charge of student publications from 1931 till 1933. Yet his student years in New Zealand were marked with bitterness through three experiences: the Auckland riots of 1932; the bungle over the Rhodes Scholarship nominations in the same year; and the controversy over academic freedom of speech of 1933.

It was in 1930 that the shadow of economic depression first touched New Zealand: by 1932 it had caused widespread suffering. Yet, strangely enough, the miseries of the unemployed and their families—numbering a fair proportion of the workers of the country—were not fully realized by those fortunate enough to remain working. It was only on April 14, 1932, when the first of the Auckland riots began, that the full extent of the nation's plight became clear for all to see.

On that night, a mass meeting of unemployed at the Auckland Town Hall got out of hand. Heavy-handed police action set up violent reaction from the assembled crowd, which swept down Queen Street, breaking shop windows and looting their contents.

Powerless to restrain the mob, the police called for special constables to help them. Because of its proximity to the police station, the university was an obvious source for such recruits, and Mulgan was one of those who thus was brought into first-hand contact with the desperate unemployed.

One friend who was with him on the first night says: "We had tea together in the university cafeteria on the afternoon following the Queen Street rioting. His concern was not so much about the rioting as about what it revealed—something that he would previously have strenuously denied—that there really had been starving people in Auckland. It was the only time I ever saw him look shocked . . ." [4]

On the second night, Mulgan went as a special constable to the Karangahape Road area, where trouble was expected. With him on that occasion was his friend, "Scotchy" Paterson, who remembers how one highly articulate and physically massive member of the crowd treated Mulgan and himself to an impassioned account of the circumstances of the majority of those present, and charged the two student "specials" with thoughtlessly bolstering an unjust social system. He himself, he said, had fought in the Great War as an officer in the British Army, to make the world safe for democracy, and now, in a democratic society, he and his family were faced with starvation.

This encounter made a vivid impression on Mulgan. Professor R. P. Anschutz (his closest friend at that time on the university staff) testifies to this fact, and says, "The main event in John's life was, I imagine, his service as a special constable during the Auckland riots." [5]

From this time on Mulgan's eyes were open to the social facts involved in the rioting. He resigned as a special constable after the second night. His friend Associate-Professor J. M. Bertram recalls how Mulgan "was the first student to throw a cold douche. He held out of the whole racket, he was certainly out of it through the week." [6]

Mulgan made a strong plea to his fellow students to consider the cause of the rioters with sympathy, in a leading article in the student newspaper, shortly after the riots. [7]

The novelist D. M. Davin has summed up more effectively than anyone else the effects on Mulgan of the Auckland riots: "The sudden realisation that many of his own countrymen had been living in misery while he lived in the sun seized his imagination and his sympathies and turned his mind towards the problem that is at the root not only of his writing but of our living. The problem can be formulated in many ways. Let us say it is the problem of how men are to live together. To hear it stated is for all of us in this decade to realize at once its relevance and its difficulties." [8]

II *The Elusive Rhodes Scholarship*

In his second year at the university, Mulgan had had the unusual distinction of being nominated for the Rhodes Scholarship —at that time the principal academic award available to students for study abroad.

Mulgan's nomination was unusual because of his youth. He was nineteen years old when he went to Wellington, along with the other Auckland nominee, J. M. Bertram (who obtained one of the two scholarships awarded in that year). Bertram's account of the journey and the interview makes clear how highly Mulgan was at that stage regarded:

. . . we travelled down to Wellington together, sharing a sleeper in the Limited. The Government House interview was pleasant enough— Lord Bledisloe as chairman thoroughly living up to his nickname as Chattering Charlie, but genuinely kind and considerate and full of bonhomie. In the end, it was announced that Geoff Cox and I were elected; and Lord Bledisloe asked all the candidates in for a glass of sherry; he kept Geoff and me back at the end, and said, when John was leaving, "Young Mulgan, we'll see you back again next year!" as clear a hint as could have been given, that with another year in, and his degree completed, John Mulgan was sure of a Rhodes Scholarship.[9]

Next year, in the October following the riots, the Auckland nominations for the Rhodes Scholarship selection were announced. It was a great shock to most people who knew Mulgan when his name was not announced as one of the nominees.

It seems clear that the professorial board mismanaged the selection. In an account of the affair which he compiled after his son's death Mulgan's father laid the blame on too rigorous an adherence to a new system of preferential voting by the board.[10] Thus two comparative nonentities were sent forward for 1932. Lord Bledisloe's reaction was vehement and spectacular. In the absence of Mulgan, he refused to make any appointment at all to the scholarships for 1932, a step unprecedented before or since.

Mulgan decided to stay in Auckland, after completing his B.A. degree in 1932, in the hope that he might be awarded a scholarship in 1933. As vice-president of the students' association and chairman of the publications committee he had a good deal to occupy him in the early part of 1933. It was the year of the college's Golden Jubilee, and Mulgan was closely concerned with two of the key productions of the Jubilee celebrations.

One of these was the *Golden Jubilee Book of the Auckland University College*. Mulgan was a member of the Jubilee Book Committee, which produced a handsomely printed 93-page book of historical and personal reminiscences.

The other project which claimed a good deal of time was his authorship of the book of the Capping Revue for 1933—a skit on

Noel Coward's *Cavalcade* which used the Golden Jubilee as a pretext for a good deal of skylarking with personalities and places known to Aucklanders. The *Auckland Star* gave the piece a favorable notice, saying among other things that "the topical songs were of a standard that was always good and often brilliant." [11]

It was during 1933 that the question of freedom of speech for academic staff became a public issue, revealing clearly the extent of the gulf between old and young which Mulgan later referred to in *Report on Experience*. The rioting in the previous year had made the general public nervous about the possible infiltration of Communist agitators. The government now brought pressure to bear on the Council of the University College to control public utterances by university staff. Mr. (later Professor) R. P. Anschutz, of the philosophy department, who had written an introduction for an account of a journey to Moscow by a New Zealand woman, was named by the Director of Education to the council. A lively public controversy arose. The academic staff were at a considerable disadvantage at this stage, since they were without a permanent leader (the office of Chairman of the Academic Board went in rotation).

As vice-president of the students' association Mulgan found himself deeply involved in maneuverings which accompanied the election of a council member. The president of the students' association had signed a document supporting the reactionary candidate. Mulgan as vice-president felt it his duty—along with a number of others—to issue a statement making it clear that there was no official student support for the candidate in question. His father was convinced that this action lost him any chance of professorial board support in the Rhodes Scholarship nominations for 1933. [12]

Hence Mulgan was faced, in October, 1933, with the necessity of mortgaging his future in order to study abroad. He borrowed money from his father, and booked a passage on the "Ruahine" to London. He had been promised a place at Merton College, Oxford. Though he would be late for the beginning of the Michaelmas Term, he was determined to show that he was capable of doing well at Oxford.

III *Emigrant Undergraduate*

London looked forbidding on November 17 when "Ruahine" docked at Tilbury. "Bleak flat land with oil tanks, occasional factories, and rotten ships," he wrote home. Mulgan's uncle— Geoffrey, his father's brother—met the boat and took him to Oxford by car.

There he found the term nearly over. He was given rooms in the Fellows Quad at Merton overlooking the Fellows Garden, and was at once absorbed into an exacting routine of work, talk, recreation, and social activity which was to increase in intensity as the years passed.

After a week at Oxford, Mulgan wrote home: "It is quite the most interesting life I have lived till now . . . I seem to live in a whirl with rare intervals of peace and reflection." [13]

Various acquaintances and friends had preceded Mulgan to Oxford. There was Jack Bennett, already installed at Merton. There were also the Rhodes Scholars of 1931—Cox[14] and Bertram[15]— who gave him the friendliest of welcomes. The former, at Oriel, became a close friend, and after he went down and got a job in Fleet Street, remained in contact with Mulgan. Cox served with distinction in the New Zealand Division during the war, and wrote a good book on the Trieste campaign. He was knighted in 1965.

Another New Zealander with whom he made contact very promptly was Kenneth Sisam, an Auckland Grammar School Old Boy who had been a contemporary of his mother's at Auckland University College, a former Rhodes Scholar, and was now assistant-secretary to the Delegates of the Clarendon Press. Sisam, famous as an Old English scholar, was an Honorary Fellow of Merton. He was always kind to New Zealanders at Oxford, and had Bennett and Mulgan to tea at his handsome modern house on Boar's Hill on the first Sunday of Mulgan's residence at Merton.

The English tutor at Merton was at that time Edmund Blunden; Mulgan describes him as "a strange, dark little man—very shy and hesitant in his speech." [16] In fact he was impressed by the modesty of the renowned scholars who clustered so thickly in Oxford.

The remainder of the term passed very quickly. Mulgan grew to

know the young Englishman on his staircase better as time
passed, and found him a genial and amusing companion who became a close friend.

The vacation found Mulgan exploring London. With a base at
his Uncle Geoffrey's house in Drayton Gardens, South Kensing-
ton, he made contact with numerous literary friends of his father's
—among them Hector Bolitho, a New Zealander who was later to
collaborate with him on *The Emigrants*. Also in London was his
sister, Dorothea, then nearing the end of a visit to England, and
the purser of the "Ruahine," Mr. Colmer, who entertained Mulgan and his sister one night, in the fleshpots of Soho.

The rest of the vacation was spent with a New Zealand friend
then at Cambridge, Colin Reeve, who had rented a cottage in
Warwickshire; and finally Mulgan went for Christmas to some
aged relations at Oswestry. He wrote to his family on the eve of
his twenty-second birthday:

. . . I wish I felt as old as I did two or three years ago. I am aghast at
the high level of culture and knowledge of people younger than myself
that I meet here. Of course they can't all sail a boat or play football,
but that's not much use. However, there's time for all things and I
learn quickly . . .

The new term brought a round of lectures and tutorials, rugby
football playing, and social activity. Mulgan was tried two or
three times for the O.U.R.F.C. Greyhounds—the University Second XV. He enjoyed rugby football very much, though he wrote:
"The football is easier than what I had in New Zealand but would
be of a fair standard if everyone was a little bit fitter."

In February he wrote to his father that he had completed two
articles about life in England, and this journalistic writing was to
prove something of a habit in the next few years. Partly Mulgan
was trying to make a few pounds to ease things for himself and his
parents (many are the references to money and to his current
expenses in his letters home, and he was most conscious of the fact
that he was pushing his father's finances—never particularly
healthy—near their limit); but also he felt a genuine impulse to
write. In spite of his protestations—"It is a tremendous effort to
me to write that sort of stuff . . ."—he demonstrated great apti-
tude for the difficult task of turning out topical opinions and lively

firsthand accounts of English life, based on what he heard and saw.

In this connection his close friend Geoffrey Cox has this to say: ". . . He was in my view first and foremost a writer—and I believe it is as a writer he would have remained and developed. He had an extraordinary capacity for looking outside himself, at other people and other things, which gave him a great initial advantage as a writer . . ." [17]

The first articles Mulgan sent home were entitled "Life at Oxford." A series of three,[18] they covered his first impressions of the university. Lightly, but not exaggeratedly humorous, they provide an accurate and life-like account of settling in, meeting one's tutor, attending lectures, and the ceremonies of college admission and matriculation.

How crowded life was, is indicated by an extract from a typical letter home:

I managed to get a little work done on Sunday. Monday was really warm and fine. I went to Blunden's lecture in the morning and listened to a very irreverent demolition of *In Memoriam*. I suspect he has little sympathy for the Victorians but prefers his beloved Lamb and Coleridge. An American girl who sat next to me seemed to be rather shocked. After lunch Bennett and I went for a walk round the Meadows. They are getting excited about rowing now. The rowing men eat huge breakfasts and special dinners, the main idea being apparently to put on weight. I still think it's a silly sport. Last night was quiet, except that Bertram came round after dinner and I gave him coffee. He was full of the Austrian news that had just come through, and the Paris riots. The world is certainly moving—God knows where. The Austrian socialists seem to me to have virtually committed suicide. As for fascism here, reason tells one not to take it seriously, but the fascists one meets, the sort of hearty, hunting Indian service and Army people are so stupid. Lord Rothermere is a joke of course and Mosley is ill, but the whole business is disquieting, merely to think that *anyone* should believe in it.

Today was foggy and later dull and damp. Bennett and I went for a good walk about 7–8 miles to Godstow and the Trout Inn, came back to tea and then I worked at my essay which I will finish tonight . . . Sorry to be so brief, but there seems little to record.[19]

The Easter vacation was spent, like the Christmas one, partly in London and partly in the country. Mulgan spent a good deal of time in London visiting publishers with the manuscript of his father's novel, *Spur of Morning*—to no avail. He went to the Boat Race, attended a performance of *Wozzeck* at the Queen's Hall, and proposed the toast of "The School" at the Auckland Grammar School Old Boys Dinner.

The remainder of the vacation he divided between his friend Colin Reeve, with whom he spent a week in Sussex, a friend of his parents (a Miss Tennant who had a farm in Suffolk), and Hector Bolitho. The last-named drove him back to Oxford from his country house at Princes Risborough on April 22.

The summer term at Oxford is as a rule heavily loaded with social engagements, and Mulgan soon found, as he said, that "Summer is very much a holiday term for all except those who have examinations; even our tutors treat it as such and it is difficult to work as seriously as in the darker days."

During this term Mulgan had cause to measure the distance he had come even in so few months, from the New Zealand outlook on things. He had been sent some copies of *Tomorrow*, a "progressive" New Zealand journal, and he comments: "The average New Zealand revolutionary intellectual is a very lonely and useless figure. Having just seen *Tomorrow* I can see how futile it all is. They are out of touch with the working class and with their own class." [20]

Furthermore, his father had refused to publish in the *Auckland Star* the essays on Oxford which he had sent home: they were too irreverent. Alan Mulgan's *Home* had been an unreasoning paean of adulation of all things English. His son's questioning attitude seemed to him in bad taste. Mulgan replies moderately to his father:

As for . . . my attitude to Oxford, I cannot accept it all; it is very lovely and becoming more so in late spring. As I write I look out on the garden of elms and green lawn and colored flowers, and we have had three cloudless and windless days. But I will not subscribe to the feeling that old things are ipso facto beautiful and to be admired—only some of them are beautiful.

In Eights Week social life became just too crowded for comfort. The Australians playing cricket in the Parks; a performance of *Everyman* in Exeter Fellows Garden; dinner at High Table in

Trinity; a dance at the Merton history tutor's house in Merton Street; a visit from Uncle Geoffrey, with cousin Julia, a girl of thirteen; a lunch party which he and his neighbor, Frank Harley, gave in the latter's room; lunch with the Frank Taylors (a New Zealander who was a French don at Christ Church)—these were a few of his engagements.

Perhaps the funniest event of Eights Week was the meeting of the Bodley Club. This is how Mulgan describes it:

There is one exclusive club in Merton, the Bodley Club, limited to 24 members and devoted to being clever—amusing rather than deep. The principle is that to be elected one has to be taken along by someone as a guest to one of their fortnightly meetings, where somebody reads a paper on some out-of-the-way subject. To qualify for election one has to make a witty remark—if the club approves and there is a vacancy you are elected, otherwise not. I had been asked to go along to their meeting on Friday last, and the day before I found out that the paper, which was called "Forgotten Island" was about Pitcairn. Now as I am certainly the only man in the College who has seen it, the coincidence is curious. I told the secretary, whom I know quite well. He is an amusing little man with spectacles and an ambition to be Mayor of Doncaster, his home town. He asked me if I had any photos of it which he could use in his reply. I looked but couldn't find anything, but he helping me, came upon my New Zealand photos and said he was determined to use them. So that at the meeting he passed round a photo of the Poor Knights (showing the bow of the *Winsome*) as Pitcairn; Uncle Arthur and Mr Fraser shaking hands, as Admiral Rodwell saying goodbye to King Christian, and one of Ross Island as Pitcairn from the other side . . . I made my few remarks at times and was elected. And so to bed.[21]

IV *Long Vacation and Second Year*

For the summer vacation Mulgan obtained, through his friend Cox, a job as a farm laborer, on a large estate near Peterborough. Much of the local color of Part II of *Man Alone* has its origin in this experience.

Mulgan found the work hard for a start. "The first few days they were haymaking and went on working again after tea till half-past eight or nine. I found it damned hard, my hands blistered and I was stiff all over."[22]

He found the insight into English farming which he gained interesting enough to move him to write about the subject. Eventually he wrote a series of five articles which appeared in the *Auckland Star*.[23]

The job lasted a month. After that Mulgan divided his time between three places—Stroud, where he spent some days at the house of Sir William Rothenstein (a friend of his parents); London; and a seaside cottage at Whitby. The latter venture was a joint one: he was a member of a reading party of four Oxford and Cambridge undergraduates. Then he returned to Oxford in October.

As he settled into term in new rooms in Mob Quad the magnitude of his task and the scantiness of his means rather oppressed him.

Though doubtful of his chances of a first, he felt the pull of New Zealand, writing at this time to his father: "Cox and Bertram and myself all want to come back but we feel we must do something over here first." [24]

More New Zealanders turned up in Oxford. One was Norman Davis;[25] another Ian Milner, son of the well-known rector of Waitaki Boys' High School. Of the two, though Davis was in his own college, and Milner at New College, it was the latter that Mulgan preferred. They doubtless had a bond in the embarrassment each felt regarding his father's reputation in New Zealand. Alan Mulgan's reputation as a journalist of fluent charm, and Frank Milner's as a fervid reactionary and propagandist for the nineteenth century concept of Empire, had a similar faded and orthodox appearance.

Another New Zealander to come into residence at University College was Mac Cooper, an agricultural scientist and a good rugger forward who was later to captain the Oxford side. There were others—in fact fourteen attended a meeting in Mulgan's rooms at which it was decided to reconstitute a New Zealand club at Oxford which had long since lapsed—the Hongi Club. Cox was made president, Mulgan secretary. They decided to meet fortnightly for political (and New Zealand oriented) discussions.

Winter settled down over Oxford. There was a good deal of rugger, some visiting, and of course the two regular weekly essays —one for Blunden and one for Bryson. Mulgan was invited to a party, midway through November, to meet some Oxford women ("not very impressive, I am afraid, they all work too hard"). A constant visitor was Geoffrey Cox—"he dashes in for a minute or two and off again."

The last part of the term built up into a social whirl, as usual. The term ended frantically, and Mulgan was able to get away at last. At the "don-rag" Blunden prophesied that he was worthy of a first, so it was in an exhausted but contented spirit that he went down to Worcester, with his friend from the same staircase, Frank Harley.

At Worcester they met Colin Reeve, bought some provisions, and took the bus for White Ladies Aston and the same cottage they had come to a year before. Reeve has this to say of the reading holidays he spent with Mulgan:

John was a delightful companion on these occasions, always unselfish, invariably good-humoured and philosophical, and never gave the slightest indication that my ability was considerably less than his, though it was obvious enough to me. His conversation was full of banter and we laughed a lot. I don't often remember him talking seriously, though much of our time must have been spent in conversation, sometimes on poets and novelists, plays and literary criticism . . . He had broader and far more mature judgments than I had, and in consequence I often sought his opinions in order to help me form my own. He had, in many ways, the outlook of a man ten years his senior . . .[26]

The party broke up on December 22. Mulgan traveled first to Oxford to pick up some clothes, then to London.

Back in Oxford on January 2, Mulgan was able to review his experience of life in London. He wrote an article in which the loneliness of the capital is the dominant theme.[27] And he wrote to his sister Dorothea:

I don't think that I want to live in London. It might be better with a regular job and not so much time to think, but it tires and depresses me more than any place, and though now I have a lot of friends there and enjoy myself, it is a fairly grey background. I think colonials like you and me are faced with a conflict: there is every mental attraction over here, the stimulus of crowds and work and everything cultural, and on the other side you have an attraction which is largely physical for a simpler and more natural way of living. You don't realise till you have been here a while how much health means wealth. Nearly everybody that likes living in London goes out of it for the week-ends, and to live the suburban life when you can't do that must be grinding, to say nothing of the strata below. The English really lead very dull lives. After talking to people at college who live in London without being really wealthy, I could see how much they hated it. They make very few friends and have hardly any casual acquaintances. I think I should like to try living in a large block of flats in some casual place like New York for a while, to see what it was like. But I can feel the difference in friendliness as soon as I go from London even to a provincial town here.[28]

Since the college was still shut for the Christmas vacation Mulgan went into a room in Holywell Street, No. 16—at the Long Wall Street end, on the north side of the street. Among his Christmas mail had been another manuscript from his father. This time it was a travel book about New Zealand—the ultimate title was *A Pilgrim's Way in New Zealand*.

The book was to be published by Oxford University Press, London, and once again Mulgan found himself revising and correcting his father's work. There can be no doubt that he was seriously out of sympathy with his father's literary aims, but his letters are always polite, if sometimes slightly acid.

While the college was so empty Mulgan was able to read very usefully in the Bodleian. He also saw more than he had done of the senior fellow, H. W. Garrod, a scholarly bachelor who lived in college, and was fond of playing bridge. He valued Mulgan's company not only for his wit and his bridge-playing, but also for the vitality he imparted to everything he did. Mulgan, for his part, revered Garrod as a household name in the world of English literary studies, and found him a wise and a stimulating man to talk to.

The winter always made him feel low-spirited, and he began, towards the end of February, to feel run down. He thought it was just a temporary indisposition, but on March 6 he was attacked by severe abdominal pains which the college doctor diagnosed as acute appendicitis. The same day he was admitted to the Radcliffe Infirmary and operated on—in the nick of time.

After a fortnight in bed he was allowed up, and spent his convalescence at the home of the Taylors, in Iffley Road, a large house backing on to the Christ Church cricket field. He rapidly recovered his strength with the return of mild sunny days.

Late in March he went to Norwich and stayed with Frank Harley's family, which did him a lot of good.

After a short stay in London when he saw Cox—then beginning work with the *News Chronicle*—he took the train to Saffron Walden, in Essex, where he stayed some days with Hector Bolitho, who had just bought a house there. Bolitho offered him the chance to collaborate in a book of essays on early travelers to New Zealand. Mulgan accepted the offer, and the book, after long delays, came out as *The Emigrants* in 1939.

Then came a stay at Selsey with the Geoffrey Mulgans, a visit to Cox in London (down, in his turn, with appendicitis) and then the summer term was on—his last as an undergraduate.

Proofs of *A Pilgrim's Way in New Zealand* made life even busier than usual. But towards the end of May a weekend of frantic activity developed. The prime minister of New Zealand was visiting England for the Silver Jubilee, and the Hongi Club was to put on a dinner at Merton in his honor on May 25. Mulgan, now president, had all the arrangements to see to. As though this were not enough in itself, his friend Geoffrey Cox was, on the same day, being married at Haslemere, just over seventy miles from Oxford, in Surrey.

It says a good deal for Mulgan's organizing powers that both these functions were highly successfully stage-managed!

After this strenuous Saturday, the Hongi Club members spent a slightly less arduous Sunday showing the prime minister Oxford. Mulgan found Coates an attractive figure: "I don't think he can be clever. Half army major, the rest naivety, boyish pleasure in his position, in having dined with royalty, some assurance, blue eyes that may not mean honesty but are certainly attractive, and a confidence that could be either character or ignorance. But all charming because of being very direct and unassuming." [29]

Mulgan's papers began on a Friday, June 14, and went on, two papers per day, for four and a half days. He was calm but not overconfident. "I feel my limitations more and more," he wrote home. "My mind is not clever—or not when worked at high speed —I become heavy and obvious."

By June 20 his papers were finished, and a great sense of liberation descended. He was not sanguine over how he had done. "I feel that I got only a good second," he wrote home, "only in two papers did I feel that I was distinguishing myself." He had no time to idle, however—his father's proofs and the writing of *The Emigrants* now became urgent. The day after his examinations ended he was at work in the Bodleian on Charles Armitage Brown and Meryon.

Then till June 25 he stayed in London. Finally, quitting the stifling air of London, Mulgan took the train to Saffron Walden and put in three solid days with Bolitho working on *The Emigrants*. Between them they wrote thirty-five thousand words in this time.

Then on Thursday, June 27, came a miraculous telegram, from the secretary of the Delegates of the Clarendon Press, offering him a position for a year on probation, at a salary of £250 per annum.

V *Employed by the Delegates*

The Oxford University Press is possibly the largest publishing house in the world, but its workings appear mysteriously casual to the uninitiated. From a modest old-fashioned building in Oxford a worldwide network of agencies and warehouses is controlled by a collection of Oxford scholars—the Delegates of the Press. These men function without emolument—as a board of directors, making decisions on what books will be published. The task of running the business day by day falls to a secretariat: a handful of top executives whose job it is to advise the delegates and to get the books produced and marketed.

It was to this body that Mulgan was recruited. His immediate superior was Kenneth Sisam, a remarkable New Zealander who has this to say about the secretariat at that time:

The secretariat in 1935 consisted of a Secretary, an Assistant Secretary and a Junior Assistant Secretary. The Secretary is the link between the Delegates and all departments, so that he is largely occupied with the general business of the Press. When John joined he was R. W. Chapman, known as a specialist in Jane Austen and Johnson. The Assistant-Secretary (at that time myself) was chiefly responsible for the Delegates' learned books and authors—including their production. The Junior Assistant Secretary has a large independence in whatever part of publishing is assigned to him: he was then A. L. P. Norrington (now President of Trinity College, Oxford) with all classes of "educational" or "schoolbooks" as his department.

When John joined there was no expectation of a near vacancy in any of these posts. But we were on the look out for somebody to start training for the future, and so kept an eye on those who were finishing their University course and were not committed to one of the professions or a family business. I, of course, knew John, his parents and his Mulgan grandparents; and we could get opinions from his Merton tutors. They were favourable. The only doubt expressed was whether he had the equipment in pure scholarship required in the Secretariat, for they are "general purposes" officials who may have to deal with books and authors in any field of learning. Still, one can't have every assurance, and his name was brought before the Delegates' Finance Committee (the F.C. of the Press record) because it is thought desirable that they should approve the appointment of anybody who was likely later on to be put forward for consideration as one of the secretariat. The F.C. approved and John worked under the Assistant-Secretary, who can offer the most miscellaneous training ground.[30]

Of all the members of the secretariat of the Press, the one who was nearest in age to Mulgan was A. L. P. Norrington,[31] known familiarly as "Thomas." He writes of Mulgan at this time:

I have a clear recollection of having first met him at the London office of the O.U.P. . . . His smile was wide and friendly, but watchful, and his hand was hot! . . . I think that if we had been the same age, and I had not been, when I met him, already married and a busy husband and father, I might have got to know him really well . . . we used to talk a lot in the office, and play squash together; . . . and I think John thought I was a not entirely unredeemable member of the easygoing British bourgeoisie; but his really close friends were, naturally, younger and more adventurous than me. I remember his hopefully lending me a copy of (Albatross Edition, I expect) *Lady Chatterley*, about 1935, and when I said I wasn't very much taken with it, he told me it was, he thought, a "beautiful" book. I still don't agree![32]

Mulgan began work at the Press one Monday morning in July. He found the work absorbing and exacting, and set out to find out as much as he could as quickly as possible. He still had to work at *The Emigrants* in the evenings, a task welcome enough in the loneliness of his digs in Holywell.

On the morning of July 24 the lists of passes in the English School went up on the boards at the Examination Schools. Mulgan, and his friend Jack Bennett, were both in the First Class.

A Pilgrim's Way in New Zealand was published in August, and

Mulgan finished what was required of him in connection with *The Emigrants*. Publication of this book was held up for some time, however, through Bolitho's changing his publisher.

In September Mulgan began his custom of making weekly journeys to London on Press business. Sometimes they were more frequent, but it was a pattern that persisted right up till the war. He enjoyed these visits, though they were tiring, for they enabled him to keep in touch with his friends in London, and in particular with people like R. M. Campbell at New Zealand House, with whom he used to have long and serious discussions on current political events.

He also took to going out with an Oxford girl, Gabrielle Wanklyn, whom he had first met at a sherry party just after his finals.

Late in October he undertook the first of the regular tours of the universities which were necessary to keep in touch with potential writers of learned books. Kenneth Sisam says, "The third stage of [Mulgan's] training was to travel and visit authors outside of Oxford . . . John was good at it, with good manners and good conversation." [33]

At home Mulgan's father had left journalism and become director of talks for the New Zealand Broadcasting Service. Nevertheless, Mulgan had persevered with his approaches to his father's old paper, the *Auckland Star,* and managed to get an agreement from the editor, E. V. Dumbleton, to take a regular series of newsletters entitled "Behind the Cables," which Mulgan hoped to be able to do in the course of 1936, in collaboration with Geoffrey Cox. "I want to try and give people in New Zealand some idea of what this country is thinking and what exactly the cable news means—perhaps rather ambitious but I think it can be done." [34]

During the Lent Term of 1936 Mulgan had to reside in College in order to take his B.A. in the summer, and he was glad to avail himself of Professor Garrod's hospitality, using the dining room of Garrod's set of rooms as a study, while he had an attic bedroom on another staircase in Fellows' Quad. He was glad to be in College again. He had found life in lodgings lonely.

Understandably, at the beginning of a new year, he was thinking seriously of where he wanted ultimately to settle down. On his trips to London he regularly saw R. M. Campbell at New Zealand

House—made a point of it, in fact, with one eye on copy for the "Behind the Cables" column (which began to appear in the *Auckland Star* in March).

On January 23 he was in London and lunched with Campbell and his wife. A Labour Government had been voted in in New Zealand, and this is Mulgan's account of the talk he had on that occasion:

His wife . . . is a charming shy Scotswoman from Skye. We talked about New Zealand politics a lot—he was very hopeful—of course, his sympathies were always left although he served Coates (he admires the latter and thinks him undeservedly unpopular). He thinks Geoff and I should go back soon, full of plans, thinks Fraser and Nash will have to come to England soon. I don't much want to get my livelihood on the secretarial side of politics—otherwise it's all attractive; but I expect I shall want to stay here a year or two. Of course, most people would tell me I was a fool, if I gave up this job now or at any time. Sisam says it will be confirmed in March. I will go on the permanent staff, prospect of steady increase, a gentlemanly and independent life, both interesting and scholarly. But it means for one thing, living in Oxford almost permanently, an honourable and important position sooner or later, but you can understand what I should feel about such a life. Well, it's no use worrying now, but I want to keep in touch with New Zealand so that I can go back there some day. I'd rather go back as a journalist though.[35]

This is an interesting passage, for it illustrates very clearly how strong was the pull of New Zealand even after three years. Mulgan was beginning to become aware of the classic dilemma of the transplanted New Zealander. His colleague A. L. P. Norrington noticed his perplexity. He says, "He struck me as having, even more than most New Zealand 'expatriates' the feeling of being between two worlds: the intellectual excitement of Europe, and the 'frontier' freedom of New Zealand mountains and beaches and mobility. This produces a kind of underlying melancholy, odd though that word is, at first sight, in connexion with John . . ."[36]

The spring and summer terms brought their accustomed routine of pleasure. This time when Eights Week came round he was able to enjoy it to the full. He took Gabrielle Wanklyn to a Commemoration Ball, and they danced from ten till six. His feeling of freedom was further enhanced when he, Bennett, and Milner

were able to rent a house of their own at 5 Bainton Road, overlooking Port Meadow.

The summer holidays were spent once again in Northamptonshire working on the Abbotts' farm; after a week of this Mulgan
went to Cornwall for a week with Milner at Tintagel.

It was a disturbing time. The beginning of the Spanish Civil
War, the continuation of the Abyssinian War, the German march
into the Rhineland, brought the fascist threat into clear focus.

Then, in September, out of the blue, came an invitation from
the New Zealand Government for Mulgan to attend a session of
the League of Nations as an observer. This was a tremendous
stimulus to his interest in current politics. The Press authorities
willingly gave him leave. He hurriedly bought himself some new
clothes (including a black homburg hat which he ever after carried to London with him and donned when he entered the metropolis) and left Oxford on September 20. In Paris he spent a
night with Geoffrey Cox (who for the time was living there), went
on to Geneva the next day, and spent a fortnight attending meetings of the Assembly, and talking to the cosmopolitan diplomats
and journalists who were then to be found in Geneva.

He had to work hard when he came back, and what with winter
closing in and term beginning again, he had a busy round for the
next month. Cox was by then in Madrid, and Mulgan had for a
time to do all the "Behind the Cables" articles. He was seeing
Gabrielle Wanklyn as much as ever; she, for her part, was thoroughly in love with him, but she could not be altogether sure of
his feelings for her, since one or two other girls kept cropping up
from time to time, in the midst of the incredibly active social life
which Mulgan led.

VI *Marriage*

Suddenly, on February 14 he wrote to tell his parents that
he was going to marry Gabrielle.

I expect you'd like to know about her. Her other name is Wanklyn—
which always seems slightly funny to me—and her father was a doctor
and is dead. She's only nineteen—will be twenty in July—has rather
fair untidy hair and a pretty, boyish sort of face. She laughs a lot, is
very musical, and I think as intelligent as a woman should be. It's very
hard to describe people—I'm afraid you'll have to take her on trust,
but we are very fond of each other and I think can be happy together.

I rather want to get married soon because it will be a better sort of life and I distrust the future too much to wait for it.

When on April 7 the engagement was announced, there seemed very little time before the wedding date—July 10—in which to find a flat and generally get ready for housekeeping.

Gabrielle had left school at the end of 1934, and held a variety of jobs, mostly secretarial. She was working, at the time of the engagement, for the Oxford Nursing Federation, so that it was possible to meet, at lunchtimes and after work, to look at flats and houses.

In order to make some more money to meet the expenses of a new and larger household, Mulgan took on the job of compiling an anthology of verse for the Left Book Club. It was eventually called *Poems of Freedom.*

As well as *Poems of Freedom* he was at work on a book for the Press. It was the policy, in training a newcomer to the secretariat, to assign him a book to write and see through the press, so that problems of printing, binding, paper, illustrations, and so forth, would assume practical meaning for him, Mulgan's first assignment was a condensation of Sir Paul Harvey's *Oxford Companion to English Literature,* which was eventually published as *A Concise Dictionary of English Literature.* It was a scissors and paste job, but a fiddly one, complicated by the fact that on May 22 Mulgan was almost blinded by a violent head cold. "Gabrielle worked under my sightless—almost Miltonic—directions at the literary Companion," he wrote home. But he mended after a day or two.

The registry office wedding, and the quiet party afterwards finally went according to plan. Colin Reeve was best man; a party of about forty in all drank champagne in Mrs. Wanklyn's garden in Sandfield Road, Headington.

The bride and groom left by train for Southampton whence they crossed to Brittany. They had a wonderful holiday for three weeks at Ploumanach, on the north coast.

Then, in late August, they were installed in their flat at 110 Banbury Road. Oxford was empty, and Mulgan was able to get ahead with *Poems of Freedom* and the *Concise Oxford Dictionary of English Literature.* But guns were firing in Spain, and Mulgan himself had few illusions about the future. He wrote home: "As

for world politics, I expect that will work out to plan, fires breaking out everywhere—first the great war, now the second imperial-
ism, Germany, Italy, Japan, leading to the great civil war. I hate it
but I find it intensely interesting." [37]

During December Mulgan had a sudden drastic attack of virus
pneumonia. It passed quickly but left him rather exhausted. He
nevertheless took on a program of Workers' Educational Association lecturing in villages round Oxford.

His letters home were despondent. On February 26 he wrote:

At times I've looked forward with a sort of gloomy pleasure to the destruction of this country and its selfish intolerant ruling classes. As it
comes nearer I can see how much that might have been enlightened
and fine is going to be lost. As you look back to 1935, saw how they
sabotaged the League—rather than risk communism in Italy—how
things have got worse ever since, how the democracies throughout Europe feel themselves betrayed, the Americans turning away disgusted,
the splendid fight that the Spanish people put up going for nothing—
it isn't any real satisfaction to know that all these people will destroy
each other.[38]

In March he had another heavy bout of influenza, which
needed three days in bed to disperse it. Gabrielle was beginning
to wonder whether John, hitherto so healthy, was being affected
by her housekeeping. She admitted that her girlhood had been
devoid of any practice in cooking or sewing; and John was an
indulgent husband—he never worried if, when he came home, he
found she had been out riding her bicycle to Wytham Woods or
looking at New College Chapel, and so had no dinner ready. In
fact, he was amused and touched by the unalloyed pleasure it
afforded her to be freed from the rather circumscribed household
in which she had grown up.

By the end of March Harvey's *Companion* was safely condensed. Gollancz, possessed of the copy of *Poems of Freedom*
since January, in the inscrutable way of publishers kept silent.
In a letter to his father Mulgan comments on the multifarious
enterprises he seemed to embark upon:

I seem to be working very hard and not doing very much. The short
textbook on international affairs that Williams[39] and I were planning

has been laid aside for the moment. We all feel that things are so con-
fused and so much happening that it's an awkward moment for anything of the kind . . . I don't want to write except perhaps as a journalist to describe something one sees, or later in my life . . . I'm to be
seeing Geoff Cox in Paris at Easter and he talks of our joining again
with a third man in London to put a newsletter to a wider field. I
think that's the sort of work I want to do as much as anything. To people like myself—knowing that one isn't an artist of any kind—this
seems the time of the pamphlet and the article where the importance
of things is the importance of a political meeting, of persuading as
many people as possible in the short time that's left which side they
should be on. I hope that isn't an hysterical or short-sighted view that
would be discounted by someone with more philosophy or a longer
view of history. These do seem to me to be crisis years.[40]

All through the spring Mulgan had been at work, besides his
other literary projects, on *Man Alone,* though only his wife, and
none of his friends, suspected that he was writing a novel.

The Press had been so pleased with his condensation of the
Harvey *Companion* that they now asked him to perform the same
operation on another of their standard literary texts—Legouis'
Short History of English Literature. This was a more exacting assignment, for it involved rewriting as well as cutting.

The events leading up to Munich made the thundery summer
even more oppressive; Mulgan tried to reassure his parents: "I
don't worry very much, though I expect I should have to fight if
there was a war. I don't think this country would be sending large
expeditionary forces abroad again. Somebody sooner or later has
to show that aggressive fascism doesn't pay or else we can't go on
living." [41]

It was just at the time of the Munich crisis that Hector Bolitho
called on him for a final effort to finish off *The Emigrants*—laid
aside now since 1935—so he went to stay at Saffron Walden on
the weekend of October 15 and 16.

VII   *Unsettled Times*

Then came a couple of unsettling developments. Before Christmas Mulgan received an offer from Victor Sifton, owner of the
Winnipeg Free Press, to join his paper as European correspond-
ent. He was seriously considering this. At the same time R. M.

Campbell was trying to interest him in a post in the Department of External Affairs; but he was as disinclined as ever for this kind of change.

His perplexity is mirrored in a letter to his parents of December 20:

I suppose, in a better age, it would be foolish to leave one of the oldest and probably the biggest publishing houses in the world, when I can reasonably expect one day to be in charge of it. It is and has been a most pleasant life, with a very great deal of freedom and varied experience. But as things are moving now, life is no longer liberal or scholarly. We are going into bad times, of continued economic depression, and external threats. If the democracies are to survive they must organise and have faith. It is this and a desire to know America and Canada which have prompted me to think of the "Free Press." They are fine people, fighting a liberal battle. If it came off, I should be back here in a year or so with complete freedom to write for places like New Zealand and Australia and to watch the working out of this problem in England.

It was in April that he took Sisam into his confidence regarding his idea of becoming a journalist in the employ of the *Free Press*. To his surprise Sisam, who had received the news with his usual inscrutable calm, sent for him a day or two later and told him the Clarendon Press would very much like to retain his services; how would he feel about ultimately taking over the managership of the large, flourishing, and important New York branch?

This put a different complexion on things, and after a day or two's thought Mulgan agreed to this proposition. He planned tentatively to go to New York in September, and thought that, if the war held off, he and Gabrielle might be able to come to New Zealand for a visit in the early part of 1940.

Still, Mulgan himself was anything but hopeful about the future. "I'm afraid," he wrote in August, "that war is very very likely, a hopeless fratricidal war which—perhaps fortunately—nobody can win. We shall all go into it here recognising its inevitability but not forgetting how it was brought about and hoping to be alive to build up something cleaner out of the wreck."

In May he had begun training with the Oxford Officers' Training Corps; he and one of his Merton friends, Kenneth Maidment,[42] used to go down to the drill hall at Manor Road for instruction before breakfast every morning. In June he was commissioned with the local regiment, the Oxfordshire and Buckinghamshire Light Infantry.

Oxford social life went on with the usual frivolity of Eights Week. In June Gabrielle was pregnant. The Merton Commemoration Ball came round again, but it was hard to enjoy the gaiety of three years before.

Mulgan and his wife were separated again for summer holidays; he went to a military camp, while she went to Switzerland with her sister Sylvia.

When camp was over Mulgan felt like a break, and went across to Dieppe with Dick Anschutz (who was over on study leave from New Zealand) on August 22, spent a pleasant twenty-four hours swimming and sunbathing, and moved on to Paris on the evening of the 23rd. It was a bizarre time to be in the French capital. "The French were mobilizing and people were evacuating Paris. The French went into this war even more quietly and unemotionally than the English." So Mulgan wrote on his return.

Anschutz, who had never been in Paris before, wanted to take the last chance of seeing some of the paintings in the Louvre, so they did a prolonged tour of the Louvre and the Luxembourg, the last day before paintings were taken down and stored for the duration. The Champs Élysées were deserted. "All one saw," wrote Mulgan, "was the queer pathos of Frenchmen going to their war-posts, little groups of men at railway stations with the small bags that carry only their washing things, saying goodbye to their wives and families, no-one crying, nor cheering, only a sort of sad fatalism." [43]

Gabrielle remembers the Friday morning when their neighbor Albin Stuebs, a German refugee, said to her on the stairs, "It's started." He meant that the German army had gone into Poland. John, who had been down at the drill hall, came back home, packed a suitcase, and left for his unit.

The long, tragic chapter which Mulgan had foreseen so clearly, had begun.

CHAPTER 3

Guerrilla Fighter

AS a subaltern in the 5th Battalion, the Oxfordshire and Buckinghamshire Light Infantry, Mulgan had a variety of homes in the first five months of the war. Guard duty on an airdrome, camp in the country near Banbury, barracks at Portsmouth, then at Hayling Island: these were the successive moves made by his battalion, of which he became adjutant in October.

Gabrielle, three months pregnant, moved to Swerford in the Cotswolds where she stayed with friends in a country rectory. Periods of leave were rare and brief.

The baby was born on March 5, 1940, and Mulgan's first impressions were not favorable. He wrote to his parents, "The child seems to be strong and this may compensate for its undoubted ugliness. It has a huge mouth, hands and feet as might be expected and a large head . . ."

In late April Gabrielle and Richard moved to Princes Risborough, to share a house which Geoffrey Cox's wife had taken.

Again, from time to time, it was possible for Mulgan to see his wife and child: but not often. When the fall of France was imminent, Mulgan decreed that Gabrielle and Richard must sail for Canada. Though it was difficult to get a passage, and impossible to take more than £10 in cash, Mulgan was confident that his Canadian journalist friend Grant Dexter would be as good as his promise and look after the young mother and child.

Ten days before his wife and child sailed, Mulgan's unit was suddenly moved to Northern Ireland. A long two years of garrison duty lay ahead of him. Preparations for the journey and final arrangements had to be undertaken by Gabrielle alone.

On June 28 Gabrielle sailed from Liverpool on the "Duchess of Richmond," with Richard in a wicker basket. She had said good-bye to John on the telephone; she was never to see him again.

I *Garrison Duty*

Of the two years Mulgan spent in Ireland little need be said. As adjutant, he had a busy and responsible time. The unit moved about a good deal: in the first year from Antrim to Coleraine, and from there to Castlerock. But a settled and not unpleasant routine was quickly established. Training and maneuvers occupied most of the time, but there were congenial homes with pleasant hosts in the vicinity; golf, rugby football, and swimming; and occasional spells of leave in England (where Mulgan went four times in all).

As time went by, and his job called for less thought and concentration, Mulgan experienced a growing sense of unease. The war news got steadily worse. The New Zealand Division was in action in Greece and Crete; but all life seemed to hold for him was an indefinitely prolonged future of training and barracks.

His melancholy was intensified by the letters he received from his wife. She found the life of a refugee in Canada—without money or home—intolerable; went to the U.S.A. in December, 1940, to stay with her cousin in Boston, where she managed to earn enough money to take her across America by train, and then by Matson liner to New Zealand. This journey she made in March, 1941, when Richard was just a year old.

Two months later Mulgan was promoted to Major, and wrote: "It is going to be very interesting in England and I am glad I am going to see it, you can credit it all to experience, having waited a long time to see the world move the way we knew it was moving. The great thing is to survive so that you can use your experience. I have very strong feelings about this so I think you can rely on me." [1]

After Hitler marched on Russia, Mulgan wrote to Gabrielle: "You see, if I'm being really honest, I don't believe in a quick end to this war and a plain peace and anything like our old way of life again. The issues are too big, the material forces too great." [2]

In the same letter he announced that he had had his name taken off the staff list "since I couldn't face the idea of being a staff officer unless I knew something about war."

The inevitable result would be, he knew, a posting abroad. But it did not come for a while. First there was a period of seven weeks in a school for senior officers near Devizes. Mulgan wrote: "About a hundred majors here which you can guess is not an invigorating sight. Half of them are solid old boys who have worked their way steadily through the army and look a little askance at amateurs like me."

The course ended in February, 1942. Then came a further period of intensive maneuvers, in the spring and summer; but at the end of May a posting to the Middle East arrived for Mulgan. He was to be second-in-command of an infantry battalion from a different regiment, just proceeding abroad.

II *The Western Desert*

A long and wearisome sea voyage was the prelude to a hasty period of equipping and training. Then, in August, 1942 Mulgan found himself in the front line at Alamein alongside the 2nd New Zealand Division. He makes clear in *Report on Experience* how moved he was to rediscover his countrymen in the Western Desert. To his parents he wrote: "I enjoyed being beside the New Zealanders more than I can say. They are more adult in war than the English and being all intelligent amateurs and civilians are uninhibited by this empty professionalism which is our curse."

Mulgan's battalion went into the line just when Rommel was mounting his last strong bid to break into the Nile Delta. Their first task in action was a night attack on Rommel's exposed flank. Mulgan as second-in-command was left out of battle, but he quickly discovered that the battalion had been badly handled by the commanding officer, who fortunately left soon after. He was replaced by a highly competent officer who brought the battalion successfully through the breakout and pursuit at the Battle of Alamein in October, after which the battalion was ordered back to refit, and then posted to the Tenth Army in Iraq.

Mulgan thought at this stage of joining the New Zealand Division; but the officers of his own unit persuaded him to stay. He wrote to his wife, in March, 1943: ". . . at this stage of the war I had better remain English . . . Life with the New Zealanders would be simpler, more direct, much more efficient. But with all their faults, as they say, I like the English and will I expect be working and living with them after the war, and had better stay now, a man with two countries liking a part of both of them."

But this intention was frustrated by the transfer of the commanding officer and the arrival of the third colonel to command the battalion since their departure from England. Mulgan very quickly formed the view that this man was incompetent and that if he were to take the battalion into action the result would be disaster. He therefore had a private conversation with him in which he suggested that the colonel should ask for a transfer. He remarks, "I don't know what I expected, but probably that I should be put under arrest."

The colonel, however, did nothing but thank him courteously for talking so frankly, invite him to come in whenever he felt like it, and shake him warmly by the hand. Mulgan was not to be deterred. He composed a letter "in grave Johnsonian English, the kind of balanced periods that happily still survive in King's Regulations," which he dispatched to higher authority. It was an unprecedented step to take, but miraculously it succeeded. Mulgan's resignation was accepted, and the colonel was shortly afterwards transferred elsewhere.

So, in May, 1943, Mulgan found himself in Cairo without a job. When he was offered the chance of parachuting into occupied Greece as a British liaison officer with SOE (Special Operations Executive, known in the Middle East as Force 133) he accepted.

III *Into Greece*

He spent the summer in preparing for his hazardous enterprise —first at Kubrit in the Canal Zone, handling small boats, then at the Special Operations Executive training school in Haifa.

Here trainees were taught such things as the Greek language, survival techniques, how to handle enemy small arms, and something about the history and customs of Greece.

The situation of the Resistance in Greece was, and continued to be, unique among the occupied countries because of the internal tensions between rival Greek political factions. These tensions overrode the enmity felt for the occupying forces, and made matters difficult for allied forces which were dropped in Greece in order to foster resistance to the Germans.

Actually, the nucleus of a military mission had been in Greece for nearly a year—since, on the last day of September, 1942, a handful of British officers and N.C.O.'s (including three sapper officers) under the command of Lieutenant Colonel E. C. Myers had been parachuted into the mountains of Roumeli in order to carry out sabotage on the German supply lines. The major target was the single-track railway which ran south from Salonica across the plain of Thessaly, and then through the rugged mountains of the Parnassus, Giona, and Oiti groups. After bitter hardships and difficulties they succeeded in blowing up the great Gorgopotamos Viaduct, after which they made their way to the west coast, expecting to be taken off by a British submarine. However, the navy had recently lost too many ships in similar episodes, and a submarine was not forthcoming. The officers were now told that they were expected to remain in Greece and set about encouraging the Greeks to form guerrilla bands for the purpose of harrying the Germans. This they did, during the long, hard Greek winter, maintaining contact with G.H.Q. at Cairo and arranging for drops of arms and equipment, which they then apportioned to Greek resistance fighters. Finally, in August, 1943 the British officer in charge of the Kharditsa area managed to construct an airstrip, in the mountains near the resort town of Neraida. A Dakota landed there, and brought out those officers who wished to come. One of these was Denys Hamson, whose book *We Fell Among Greeks*[3] is a lively and honest account of his year among the mountain bands.

John Mulgan went into Greece, then, with the second wave of British officers and men who were to work with the Greeks to make things difficult for the Germans. The organization was now much more efficient than it had been, and those who arrived in Greece knew what was awaiting them. Since May, planes had been making a routine of dropping supplies and had become very good at the job.

Mulgan landed in Greece on the day that Colonel C. M. Woodhouse (commander of the Allied Military Mission) induced the Italian Pinerolo Division, ten thousand strong, to come over to the *andartes* (Greek guerrilla fighters). The armistice with Italy had been signed on September 3, 1943, and warned of this contingency, British officers had made contact with the Italian commander, General Infante.

Mulgan landed just outside Trikkala on September 12, and was plunged straightway into a situation that he found absurd, unreal, and tragic in its implications. The original officers of the Allied Military Mission had been reinforced from time to time, so that by now there was a British liaison officer in contact with Greek resistance forces in every area of Free Greece.

IV *The Aim of ELAS*

Apparently it took some time for British officers to realize the true aims and purposes of the resistance groups comprising ELAS. From the extraordinary similarity of organization encountered wherever guerrilla leaders were met, it eventually dawned on the English that some five or six different organizations, ostensibly separate, were really controlled by KKE, the Greek Communist Party.

The only other force of any note in the resistance was the movement known as EDES, which also took the field in the Greek mountains in the summer of 1942. Its military leader was General Zervas. In the beginning, EDES had functioned as a republican liberation movement. Zervas, a colorful figure, had real talents of leadership and real strength of will. But the monolithic power of the ELAS organization edged him further and further into a position right of center, and finally into alignment with the monarchist cause. The operation against the Gorgopotamos Viaduct was the one and only time that EDES and ELAS worked together. That they did in fact do so on that occasion is a remarkable tribute to the powers of diplomacy of Colonel C. M. Woodhouse. Woodhouse says of EDES: "It was a miscellany of negatives; the principal one of which was anti-communism." [4] In March, 1943 Zervas on his own initiative pledged EDES (till then vaguely republican in sympathies) to the cause of King George of the Hellenes. The most influential result of this move took place six months later, when, spurred by the belief that Greece was on the brink of liberation, ELAS attacked EDES and so precipitated a civil war in the mountains of Free Greece.

Mulgan relates how, on his first day in Greece, September 13, 1943, he watched the Italian troops evacuating Trikkala and the Germans moving in to occupy the town. "In the confusion and excitement we nearly found ourselves left there to meet them, but met instead a middle-aged Greek who claimed to be a general and sat with him on a shadeless hill over Trikkala watching the German column move along the road." [5]

The Pinerolo Division was never permitted, by the ELAS leaders, to move as a unit against the Germans. By trickery they split up the Italian formations and disarmed their members. The arms thus gained were rapidly turned, not against the Germans, as the

British officers were hoping and exhorting, but against fellow Greeks—the members of Zervas's EDES.

However, so far from Greece being evacuated by the Germans and occupied by the Allies, the unexpected now happened. The German forces, having lulled ELAS into a sense of false security, "turned into the mountains from east and west, and rent the resistance to ribbons at will." [6]

The village in which Mulgan's first headquarters was situated, Kastania, lay in the mountains to the west of the Plain of Thessaly. As he says in *Report on Experience:* "From Kastania, where we were living, a motor road, winding and difficult, went down to Kalambaka. From the hillside above the village you could look down this road to the valley above Kalambaka . . . We had artillery and machine guns, battalions of men, and even a telephone line connecting us with the fighting front. I never saw any of this except on a map, and one of the guns afterwards and a few of the *andartes*, but this is the way it looked from the village of Kastania up in the hills in that late October sunshine." [7]

The dream-like sensation of walking round in an enemy-held country was strange at first. There was a great deal of talking and planning. One of the foremost problems was the feeding of the Italian troops who had surrendered. Though General Infante had been assured that ELAS would assume responsibility for provisioning the Italians, it soon became apparent that their attitude was one of callous indifference. Lieutenant Colonel A. Edmonds, senior British liaison officer at this time, quotes Tasso, an ELAS commander, as saying to him, "They can suffer something of what I had to suffer returning from Albania." And Ares Veloukhiotis, the fanatical communist general, remarked to Edmonds, "They can all starve for all I care." In actual fact the British managed by one device or another to keep alive seven thousand out of the original ten thousand Italians.

It was in the last days of October that the ferocious German drive against the Greek guerrillas developed. After duping the ELAS leaders into thinking that German forces were evacuating Greece, and so that the time had come for ELAS to fight their fellow Greeks in EDES, the Germans mounted strong offensives against the areas known to be harboring guerrilla fighters. Mulgan witnessed such a drive on Kastania, and relates his baffled amazement when he realized that, in face of the German advance, the *andartes* were simply going to retreat and temporarily disband. "I still did not understand that there was not going to be any fighting, and that we were all going away and merely leaving the village and the people in it to make the best peace they could with the Germans." [8]

This first encounter with a German sweep was a sobering experience. The village of Kastania, where Mulgan was at the time, is connected by a very poor and winding single-track road to the main Trikkala-Ioannina highway. Germans had never before penetrated as far as the village, but they must have had definite information that the British Military Mission had an H.Q. there, for they pressed on to the village itself.

It seems that this initial encounter with Germans was met by Mulgan with an ill-judged decision not to move at the first warning of the approach of a motorized unit. The result was disastrous, for he lost, in his own words, "our half-evacuated wireless set, several thousand dollars' worth of paper money, and all the winter clothing and cognac we had so carefully stored." [9]

There ensued an exhausting trek southeast through the mountains to Pertouli, where the H.Q. of the British Military Mission was situated. With Mulgan on this trek was Major "Rufus" Sheppard, who had been dropped onto Mount Olympus on January 3, 1942, and the appearance of their party at Pertouli is thus related by a British liaison officer, Major Michael Ward, who was there at the time: "The same evening that I arrived at the mission hut in the fir forest, John Mulgan and 'Rufus' Sheppard staggered in looking absolutely worn out. They had marched across country with their wireless operator and other members of their 'station' after having been surprised by a sudden German raid . . ." [10]

Mulgan was to have many close brushes with the Germans in subsequent months, but never again was he caught in such a risky situation as on this first occasion.

He was next appointed commander of Area 3—that is, the area bounded by Othris to the east (containing the Almuros-Lamia road); and the mountainous area of Roumeli west of the Lamia-Dhomokos railway line. He set up his headquarters in a little village deep in the Timfristos mountains, called Fourna. This village was at that time inaccessible to wheeled transport, though good mule tracks connected it with Rendina and the Karpenisi road. Here there was a wireless set which had contact with Cairo. On the other side of the railway, on Mount Othris, a sub-area post under the command of Major Ian Selby Nevill, had two young Royal Engineers officers on its strength. These were Lieutenant Kenneth Walker and Lieutenant A. C. Campbell. The latter officer's special responsibility was the German airdrome at Almuros, on the far side of Mount Othris.

A forward station was set up south of Fourna and closer to the Sperkheios Valley, in a village called Tsouka, in the hills overlooking, and midway between, the two small towns of Makrakomi and Pirgos. From here a regular army officer—Major Pat Wingate of the Royal Engineers—kept the railway line under surveillance, and trained Greek *andartes* in the use of explosives. Wingate had two assistants—Sergeant Lou Northover, a member of the New Zealand Division who had been on the loose in Greece since the 1941 campaign, and Corporal J. M. MacKay of the Long Range Desert Group.

Northover was a tough and rugged New Zealander who had spent two hard winters in Greece, and had been forced into threatening peasants with violence in order to obtain food. Word of his exploits had reached the British Military Mission, and Lieutenant Colonel Woodhouse had ordered him to report himself to Mission Headquarters, in 1943. He had turned up at Gardiki, with a German deserter—an Alsatian from an airdrome unit, for whose bona fides he confidently vouched. Northover, who survived the war and now lives in Auckland, became one of Mulgan's hard-core assistants; he himself is full of admiration for Major Pat Wingate's coolness and expertise with explosives.

Major Wingate himself has this to say about Mulgan's assumption of command in Area 3: "I viewed the prospect of another 'colonial' with gloom. Then he arrived. His easy confident manner, his broad grin and understanding ways won us over immediately. Morale in the station went up and never slipped back again."

V *Preparation for Sabotage*

The immediate objective of the British Mission was the preparation of a detailed plan of sabotage which should prevent the Germans from withdrawing their troops intact from Greece, when the time came for them to go. The difficulty was that the ELAS commanders were unwilling to commit the forces at their disposal to systematic guerrilla warfare against the Germans. The lot of a B.L.O.[11] was exasperating, in these circumstances. Some, like Major W. S. Jordan, whose fellow officer, Lieutenant Arthur Hubbard, was accidentally shot by an ELAS band, maintained that no good could come of arming and encouraging an organization whose covert purpose was the political domination of Greece in the postwar period. Others, like Brigadier "Eddie" Myers, thought that the short-term objective of winning the war justified the harassment of the Germans and the encouragement of the civilian population which supplying and recognizing ELAS involved.

Myers had left Greece by airplane before Mulgan went in. His defense of ELAS gained him the displeasure of the Foreign Office, as he outlines in his book,[12] and he never returned, his place as head of the British Military Mission being taken by Lieutenant Colonel C. M. Woodhouse. This officer was successful in persuading SOE (Cairo), the H.Q. of Force 133, that continued support of ELAS was essential to the Allied cause.

So it was that, after the disastrous events of October, into which Mulgan had been so rudely plunged, the resistance in Greece prepared and reorganized for Operation "Noah's Ark," the code name given to the sabotage plan which was to go into effect whenever the Germans showed signs of evacuating the country.

Mulgan was fortunate in the ELAS formation with which he had to work so closely. This was the 16th East Thessaly Division. Its members, about fifteen hundred strong, came mostly from the neighboring towns of Volos, Almuros, and Larissa, and were in general more intelligent and resourceful than the villagers of Roumeli. They were under the command of an exceptionally gifted former Venizelist colonel, Costa Tsamakos, with whom Mulgan's relations were most cordial. He speaks, in *Report on Experience,* of "the long snow-bound hours when we cheered each other in Fourna, passing *tsippouro*—a lower-class cousin of *ouzo*—across the fire and exchanging reminiscences."

Since no other resistance bands were operating in this area, the 16th Division were prepared to be friendly to members of the Mission. On the foundation thus created, Mulgan was able to build a superstructure of cooperation and trust which was probably unique in the whole of Greece. Lieutenant Colonel Nick Hammond comments: "The policy of ELAS was definitely to fa-

vour one BLO . . . (I had been so favoured in Macedonia) and
it made it more difficult for such a Liaison Officer to view ELAS
as suspiciously as the other officers did." [13]

The initial months spent in making his area shipshape involved
many exhausting journeys by foot and on horseback. The wireless
station had to be set up at the sub-area station on Mount Othris,
on the other side of the main road and railway. Since road and
railway were under regular German patrol, crossings had to be
attended with some caution. Major Michael Ward thus describes
a journey with Mulgan:

About the 13th or 14th December, 1943, I was making for the east
coast in order to board a caique for Turkey. On arriving one evening
at Fourna, near Karpenisi, I was told that Mulgan was in the vicinity
and was about to leave in the same direction as myself. I managed to
contact him by phone and we arranged to meet the following evening
at Leondari on the western edge of the Thessalian plain prior to crossing it by night. After a twelve-hour slog I arrived at Leondari to find
Mulgan, his interpreter Paul Contomichalos, and others of his group
just finishing their evening meal in the local tavern. After dark we
mounted horses and rode in intense cold across the marshy plain, stop-
ping at about midnight to change horses and drink several shots of raw
local spirit. We were over the plain by 4 A.M., and then climbed up,
on foot once more, into Mt. Othris and kept going till about 6 P.M.
when we reached the village of Filiadhon where Mulgan then had his
H.Q. . . . I left next day for Mt. Pelion.

On Mulgan's powers of endurance, Paul Contomichalos, his interpreter (who remained with him continuously from his arrival
in Greece until they both went to Cairo in October, 1944), has
this to say:

John Mulgan loved his job, riding or walking across the mountains
of Central Greece and was, I believe, one of the most popular Allied
officers in this region, both with the Greeks and with his own men.

He was always even-tempered, gentle, and took everything in his
stride, whether he was under fire or weathering the rigours of mountain storms. He was a terribly tough walker and could go on for hours
up and down mountains without feeling tired.

Pat Wingate recounts his first operation with Mulgan thus:

It took place a day's march away from my out-station, on the Thessaly plain. Except for a short rest before dark we were on the move from early morning to just before dawn the next day. Then, after barely two hours rest, he had me on the move again, just the two of us, to get back to his own H.Q. up in the Pindus Mountains. It took us ten hours hard riding and towards the end I was falling asleep on my horse, but John seemed able to go on for ever.

The chief objectives in Mulgan's area were the main north-south road and the Lamia-Larissa railway. In addition there was a narrow-gauge railway running east and west and linking Volos, Farsala, and Kharditsa, and supplying the German garrisons in the plain of Thessaly. Other targets were the coast road Lamia-Almura-Volos, and the Xinia chromium mine narrow-gauge railway.

Of these communication routes, the main railway was the most vulnerable. Two brilliant demolitions—of the Gorgopotamos and Asopos viaducts—had shown the Germans in Athens how easy it was to wreck their contact with Europe. The cutting of the Gorgopotamos Viaduct had created a six-week gap in the supplies which were vitally needed about the time of the Alamein break-out; the Asopos demolition had coincided with the Allied invasion of Sicily and had helped to convince the Germans that Greece itself was to be invaded.

Hence the railway line, when Mulgan began his operations, had armed guards on all main bridges, tunnels, and stations. Usually of about a platoon in strength, the guard forces occupied concrete defense positions—in many cases a two-storied pill-box—and were usually protected by wire and anti-personnel mines.

Where heavier protection was needed, detachments of up to company strength, with heavy weapons, would be stationed. Over the forty-one miles of rail between Lamia and Dhomokos, where the line debouched into the plain, one thousand German troops were on guard duty.

To carry out successful sabotage against a route so heavily guarded called for considerable daring, and—perhaps even more necessary—cool and thorough planning. By this time supplies of various kinds were coming in with some regularity—food and clothing by caique from Turkey to the east coast, whence they would be carried by mule train or by human porters (usually women from the mountains) to their destination. Explosives and other military stores would come by air. Sorties began to Area 3 in March, 1944 and averaged four a month.

The plan for "Noah's Ark" was brought back from Egypt on January 10, 1944, by Lieutenant Colonel Arthur Edmonds, who parachuted on to the Anatoli dropping ground and then made his way to Viniani, where Colonel Woodhouse and Major Gerry Wines (an American officer) now constituted the joint commanders of the Allied Military Mission. There he found a group of Poles, deserters from the German Army, who were helping to recover the supplies dropped by English planes for the Mission, and to keep at bay the ELAS troops who were so apt to spirit away the supplies for their own purposes.

The initial ordering of his area, which involved long and arduous journeys such as Michael Ward described, took up for Mulgan much of the months of December and January. In the latter month General Tsamakos cooperated with him to the extent of making available a small picked force of forty men to be trained in guerrilla warfare and demolition. This concession—and it was one not made in any other region—of placing Greek *andartes* under the direct command of a B.L.O. was in part a tribute to Mulgan's powers of persuasion. As Pat Wingate puts it, "He had a remarkable understanding of and patience with the Greeks, who could be more than infuriating at times. He never asked of them more than they could accomplish, but pushed them along gently and built up their morale and confidence in themselves."

The task of persuading ELAS commanders into some form of cooperation was assisted by the so-called Plaka Agreement which on February 27, 1944, brought to an end the civil war which had gone on, fitfully but savagely, since the previous October. EDES and ELAS agreed on a demarcation of territory under their control, and simultaneously pledged their assistance to the preparation and execution of "Noah's Ark."

Through the month of March the work of training and instructing Poles and *andartes* went on. Pat Wingate, Lou Northover, and Corporal J. M. MacKay achieved great success with their Greek trainees. In fact the spirit that their efforts generated ultimately caused these men to be regarded somewhat askance by the ELAS command. Pat Wingate says: "The detachment became so keen and co-operative under John's guidance that they were looked upon with considerable suspicion by their own high commander.

Most of them were changed over during the summer to prevent them becoming too indoctrinated with our 'monarcho-fascist' ideas. Even so, in September, when the liberation of Greece was obviously drawing near and the ELAS attitude towards us was hardening, the detachment commander told John that if and when orders came for him to arrest us, he would give us a warning, so that we could get away."

Even with the training and the regular life which the *andartes* led at Tsouka, time still hung heavy. Pat Wingate says: "Conversation and drink were our sole relaxations and we indulged freely in both. Luckily, to get anywhere, we had to walk, and the exercise soon sweated the alcohol out of us."

VI   *The Rail and the Road*

With the advance of spring and the increasing possibility of moving round unobserved and of camping in the open, Mulgan thought the time had come to test out his men's training and accustom them to operational life. He therefore arranged a number of operations against the main railway line. The two most successful were both carried out by officers from the sub-area station on Mount Othris.

Kenneth Walker led an operation in the extreme north of Area 3, where the railway, after crossing the Thessaly plain, turns to go northeast to Larissa, after crossing the Peneios River. It was an area which was less heavily guarded than the Lianokhladi-Dhomokos stretch nearer home, and an operation there might have the effect of deceiving the Germans over the location of likely future blows.

Walker blew up a troop-train with a full complement of German soldiers, killing or injuring one hundred and fifty.

On the branch narrow-gauge line to the Xinia chromium mine, Major Nevill blew up a train and destroyed the engine and sixteen wagons, killing four Germans.

These successful operations brought stern reprisals from the occupying troops. Mulgan began to realize that the real heroes of the Greek resistance were not the *andartes* but the people of the villages, who suffered reprisals and yet continued to support the underground forces. *Report on Experience* shows how acutely he felt the plight of the Greek civilians, and although he did all he could to help them, by distributing food, money, and clothing as they became available, the tragic reality of civilian suffering was a specter that dogged all his work in Greece. How far-reaching his efforts were can be judged by the fact that, twenty-two years after the event, villagers in Palaia Yannitsou and Kaitsa gratefully remembered the field-kitchens Mulgan set up and the food he procured, both from the Greek countryside, and from air-drops from Egypt, to feed the homeless.

Now the Germans took revenge by shooting hostages. Mulgan mentions in *Report on Experience* his memory of the village above Dhoxara where, on one of his first trips, people were turned out of their beds in order to accommodate his party, and where "there was hot milk and fresh eggs and bread for us before we moved on. There was a little man there, the village schoolmaster, who organised it all. He had a wizened, small face and kept making jokes that I couldn't understand . . . The Germans took seventeen men from the village and shot them by the railway line. The only one whose name I knew on the list was the little schoolmaster, but I expect there were others from among those who had been kind to us. It wasn't a very big village." [14]

But the operations of April were only a prelude. In May Mulgan led a large scale effort against the railway. At Dranitsa, well to the north of his area, a southbound goods train was derailed, looted, and burned. Nearer home the Lamia-Dhomokos road was ambushed on five occasions in this month. As a result of these enterprises five trucks were captured, thirty Germans killed, and the officer commanding the Dhomokos garrison was captured.

It was in June that a force of Americans was landed in Greece. One of them, a medical sergeant, has clear memories of Mulgan. "He spoke easily, almost purring; his broad, strong features belied his nice sense of humor. One could sense his qualities of leadership. He had complete emotional stability; I never saw his facial expression change, in all the many months and the varied situations we found ourselves . . . He could get the most out of everyone." [15]

VII *Engagement at Kaitsa*

The operation remembered most vividly by Sergeant Borgmann is the attack on Kaitsa railway station. This small station was a junction for the main Lamia-Dhomokos line and the branch line which ran to the Xinia chrome mine. The name it bears on maps is

Perivoli. Mulgan was reconnoitering the railway in the vicinity of the village of Kaitsa—about a mile from the station—which had already been burned twice by the Italians, when he was approached by a deputation. As he says himself: "The priest who led it was a friend and as smooth a politician as you would care to meet. The villagers who came with him were saddened and hardened. They had the look of all peasant Greeks, of men who don't expect much fun but are prepared to endure. They didn't ask us to stop sabotaging the railway line, but requested modestly that if we did anything it would be on a scale comparate to the reprisals that would follow." [16] Mulgan was thus encouraged to envisage activity on a larger scale than usual, involving about a hundred men.

The object of the operation in June was to capture the station and demolish the points and the traffic control gear, so as to bring about a prolonged interruption of the traffic to the Xinia mine.

Kaitsa station was—and is—a tall two-storied structure built solidly of stone, with living quarters on the top floor for railways staff. It stands on the western side of the railway line, and has a stout stone equipment store at its northern end across a small yard fifteen feet square. The Germans were using the equipment store as a mess-room. At the time there was also a wooden hutment for guard troops to sleep in on the eastern side of the line, just a little to the north of the equipment store.

Mulgan divided his force into two. The majority of the *andartes,* under their own officers, were to attack from the east and capture the wooden barrack. The Poles and Americans with some *andartes,* led by Mulgan himself, would attack from the west and capture the station buildings. The signal for the synchronized attack was to be a green flare.

The little force had a long approach march by day from Palaia Yannitsou through steep mountain paths, and had its evening meal at sunset near a small church. Then the two parties separated, in the dusk, the *andartes* to make a circuitous march across the line and towards the rising ground on the far side, before they turned northwest to approach the station. Mulgan's party had a more direct approach on a line roughly northeast. It was after midnight when the green flare—from the *andartes* group—gave the signal for the attack to begin.

What Mulgan and his men did not know was that a German

armored train was waiting in a siding about half a mile north of
the station itself. It had approached very quietly, under cover of
darkness, from the north.

The Germans in the garrison of the station (numbering forty in
all) were also on the alert. Careless talk by the Greeks had given
the Germans an inkling that something was going to happen at
Kaitsa.

Consequently, in the words of Sergeant A. Borgmann, the
American medical sergeant who accompanied Mulgan's party,
when the flare went up, "All hell broke loose . . . I saw Major
Mulgan in the dim moonlight vanish into what I was sure no-one
could survive—a devastating fire from field guns, mortars, and
machine guns." Lou Northover's comment was similar: "I thought
John had had it that time."

Mulgan's party divided, by a prearranged plan, the smaller half
to take the equipment store by storm, while Mulgan himself and
the larger group rushed the station building and demolished the
signals equipment.

His smaller party did indeed reach the storehouse, and throw
several grenades through the windows. A strong reaction came
however from the troops inside. Small arms fire and grenades
held off the party for some minutes.

Mulgan himself got into the station, but he was alone. The reason was that the Germans in the hut across the line had the en-
trance to the station buildings covered by their field of fire. The
andartes group, attacking from the east, surprised them, however.
They managed to get right up to the hut unobserved, and then
put several grenades through the windows. A fierce fire fight between these two groups ensued, but the *andartes* kept on bomb-
ing the hut, to such good effect that every German in it was killed.

Unfortunately, they did not know this, and there was not the
time to find out, for the armored train had by now appeared, glid-
ing down the line with streams of tracer bursting from its slitted
boxcars. In a matter of seconds the situation was reversed. Several
andartes were cut down by the thick pattern of fire. Mulgan in the
station building seized the fact that he might be trapped, and got
out in the nick of time. His small group had succeeded in killing
some ten or twelve of the defenders of the storehouse, but the
survivors were still firing. The appearance of the armored train
brought the whole attack to a standstill.

The parties withdrew, carrying their dead and wounded, and leaving a screen of covering fire till the majority were on their way. Losses were heavy. Fifteen men were dead, thirty wounded. Among the dead were two young Greek regular army officers, who had been with the *andartes* attacking the barrack hut.

VIII *Reinforcements*

This setback did not interrupt the operations which went on in Mulgan's area through June and July. The narrow gauge railway across the Thessalian plain, from Volos to Kharditsa, was repeatedly attacked. Eventually, in July, the last locomotive left on this line (which was the chief means of supplying the German troops in the plain) was destroyed; and the line was then inoperative until after the liberation.

The spirits of the Force 133 members in Greece were raised in late July by the arrival of a detachment of the Raiding Support Regiment—forty men in all, who came from Epirus, in the west of Greece, and who were briefed by Lieutenant Colonel Nicholas Hammond, at his H.Q. at Mezilo in the mountains west of the Sperkheios Valley. Hammond remarks, "John Mulgan was given the first detachment, because he was still on good terms with ELAS and he could attack the main line most readily." [17]

But before the English troops landed, a group of twenty Americans had joined their four compatriots (from the Medical Corps) who had dropped in June.

The example of these disciplined regulars spurred some of the *andartes* to a desire to emulate them. Pat Wingate's engineer *andartes* had been trained to a high pitch of efficiency—their record of sabotage is testimony to that. But there was no corresponding force of *andartes* which could be relied on for firm and resolute defensive fighting; so that up to the present hit-and-run tactics had been the precarious norm.

Now Mulgan set on foot the training of a commando band of *andartes*, eighty strong. It is a tribute to his diplomacy and tact that these troops—all volunteers—were supplied, fed, and armed by the Military Mission, and though they took their orders from their own Greek officers, they were in fact almost indistinguishable from the British and American troops in fire power and fighting capacity. Almost every man had an automatic weapon—a bren or a tommy-gun—and they developed a high sense of pride in their formation.

On the western side, in the Goura sub-area, Ian Nevill carried out a similar program of training; and the results there were equally good.

Midway through the month of July these newly-formed commandos were given a chance to show their paces. A particularly impudent operation was planned, which amounted to tweaking the nose of the Lamia garrison.

A bare ten miles from Lamia, where the main line first left the relative security of the valley and penetrated the first line of foothills, was a small tunnel, near the village of Stirfaka. By clever timing and great daring the *andartes* succeeded in blowing this tunnel so as to trap in it a goods train, proceeding south and fully loaded. Once trapped, the train was set on fire and totally destroyed.

Within a few days, at the extreme northern end of Mulgan's territory, the *andartes* of the Othris region, combining with their fellows from Pelion, and numbering over two hundred in all, engaged the German garrison of the town of Velestinon, only ten miles east of Volos. They were successful in capturing several pillboxes, and they inflicted heavy casualties on the German troops, who were forced out of the road and rail defenses into a central fortress area. The *andartes* held control of the road and rail for almost two days, until German reinforcements from Volos fought their way through to relieve their companions.

Exploits such as these by *andartes* were rare at any time; in most parts of Greece they were unknown. But by the end of July acts of sabotage were occurring nightly on some part of the road or rail in Mulgan's area.

IX   A Valley Laid Waste

The infuriated Germans retaliated early in August. Mulgan describes their operations in these words: "By late July we knew we had earned more than a common retribution, and reports of S.S. troops gathering in Lamia told us that it was near at hand. They drove in below us, and the fabric of partisan divisions collapsed as it always had collapsed and always would. From Old Yannitsou we did some sporadic shooting, but the Germans were engaged on reprisal and concerned themselves little with military objectives that involved clearing us back from the railway line." [18]

The Germans in fact concentrated two thousand S.S. troops in Lamia, and the object of the drive up the Sperkheios Valley, which began on August 7, was punitive rather than military. The maximum of destruction with the minimum of fighting was the obvious wish of these troops. They simply drove into village after village and tossed a phosphorus bomb into each house—thoroughly and methodically obliterating them. The population suffered only if there was resistance. But if there was, then vengeance was brutal and sudden. Mulgan tells of seeing "the bodies of two old women and one old man that I had known, shot and not killed, and left to burn in the baths, the pleasure resort of Platistomo." [19]

Mulgan was appalled and horrified by the sufferings of the civilian population. With the idea of drawing the German forces away from the program of devastation on which they were embarked, he now stepped up demolitions and sabotage from both sides of the railway. In four days, from August 9 to 13, he and his men blew up nine locomotives and forty-three coaches. They completely wrecked a kilometer of the line, into the bargain.

Though he tried hard to prevail on the *andartes* to work in with the Raiding Support Regiment troops who had by then arrived, with their three-inch mortars, their bazookas, and their Vickers machine guns, he was unsuccessful. The Greeks were suspicious of large-scale operations, and were willing to commit only small forces in nocturnal ambushes and mine-laying activities.

The intensified sabotage had absolutely no effect on the German sweep up the Sperkheios Valley. They went the whole way, as far as Karpenisi, and destroyed every village within reach. Mulgan says: "For a week we watched smoke rising over the Sperkheios Valley. It rolled up thickly and blotted out Giona from our view. Terrified villagers crowded into the hills and huddled by night round camp-fires, cherishing the few pathetic belongings that they had rescued." [20]

It was on August 19 that the S.S. troops began to return down the valley. On that night the American group attacked a troop train, just north of the ill-fated Kaitsa station. With accurate bazooka fire they knocked out both engines, and then raked the coaches with mortar and heavy machine gun fire until all answering fire was silenced.

When the salvage and repair parties appeared under heavy guard, with troop trains in attendance from Lamia, Mulgan had his British detachments of R.S.R. troops with their three-inch mortars lined up and ranged. When the repair gangs were really hard at it, and all was going smoothly, they opened up with a barrage. This was on August 24. Incensed German guard troops fanned out and came up the hills, but the mortars were gone. The Germans therefore cared for their dead and wounded, and turned to the work of making good the damage to their repair plant. It took several days.

When the line-clearing was again in full swing, on August 30, the same story was repeated, from a different direction. A battery of three-inch mortars, ranged and prepared, put down a sudden heavy barrage which further harassed the unfortunate Germans.

The Greek commando *andartes* were not idle during this time. On August 29 they mounted a very successful attack on a guard post of platoon strength near the junction station of Lianokladhi. They killed fifteen Germans, captured twelve, and found, among the booty which the post yielded, a 75-mm. field gun which they were later able to use, though unfortunately there were only forty rounds of ammunition with it.

X *German Withdrawal Begins*

The German withdrawal now appeared imminent; it had been long delayed, but the advances of the Allied forces in Normandy and in Italy now made it imperative that the Third Reich look to its boundaries. The plans concerted in February—known as "Noah's Ark"—had now to be put into effect.

Mulgan determined to use his British R.S.R. troops against the road, where mortar fire and accurate long-range heavy machine gun fire would do most damage. The *andartes* and the American troops he decided to keep for harassing the railway.

The R.S.R. troops obtained spectacular successes in their mining of the road and shooting up of truck convoys. When the Germans began withdrawing, on September 4, a convoy of between three and four hundred vehicles began to pass. The main body of the *andartes* in this area could not, however, be induced to attack. The R.S.R. troops therefore engaged the convoy from long range, with Vickers machine gun fire. They succeeded in inflicting some damage, and delayed the convoy twenty-four hours.

On the railway, there was a large demolition carried out on September 2 which closed the line for four days. Then on September 9 Mulgan blew another small bridge, which closed the line for several days. When the line was reopened he did the same thing again. In fact, between September 9 and September 18 the line was never open for more than twelve hours at a time.

On their way to Othris to begin operations against the road, the R.S.R. mortar section had sighted a German troop train. They halted it with some good shooting, then put down a barrage of bombs which killed thirty Germans and sent the Greek engine-driver running for dear life into the hills.

Mulgan was now getting so confident that on September 24 he blew the line in daylight, had the line blocked all day, damaged two trains, and with harassing fire and sniping killed several Germans.

It was too good to last, however. In the area between Lamia and Athens next to no sabotage was being carried out, and the Germans now drew troops from that area and concentrated them strongly along Mulgan's length of line, in an effort to hold off demolitions and attacks, and keep the traffic moving.

When, on September 28 and 29, Mulgan began his old tactics of shooting up repair parties who had come to where he had carried out demolitions, he suddenly found himself and his party under heavy automatic and mortar fire from a force two companies strong, which had appeared as if by magic.

This pattern was to recur. Any sabotage elicited an overwhelming response, so that the motto from now on had to be "hit and run." The last considerable success against the railway was on October 3, when a small train was derailed in a tunnel near the village of Ligaria. It was set on fire and completely destroyed.

The next day when reconnaissance parties made their regular patrols, they found that the Germans were posting a section of men every three hundred yards for the whole length of the track. This was unheard-of, and it meant that direct movement against the line was impossible from now on. The only thing to do was use what heavy weapons the *andartes* possessed, and harass the line from a distance.

The story with the road was much more encouraging. It was relatively easy to carry out a small demolition by night which would pile up the convoy by day. The R.S.R. heavy machine guns could then be used with some effect, and this pattern became the usual one.

At times the R.A.F. were summoned to strafe a congested stretch of road. This happened on September 13, when ten trucks were destroyed.

On September 16 the road was cut and traffic held up all day. It was not till the night of September 21 that traffic got going again; but it was stopped again the next day. The R.S.R. troops made a doubling movement and then attacked the same convoy further north. On this day they fired two hundred mortar bombs and five thousand rounds of heavy machine gun ammunition. No traffic moved on the following two days, and the opportunity was taken to sow mines and make further demolitions on the road.

Eventually, however, the same thing happened on the road as had happened on the railway. A pitched battle ensued between R.S.R. troops and *andartes,* and the Germans detailed to clear the road. The latter made little progress for three days. But on September 29 two battalions of infantry and a battery of 88-mm. guns forced Mulgan's men off the road.

From that point on, it was "hit and run," as on the railway. The Germans maintained a force of one infantry regiment with artillery support right through the vulnerable portion of the road. Their last party passed through late in October.

One morning in late October Mulgan rode out from Palaia Yannitsou for the last time. His runner, Dimitrio Tsoumas, rode with him. Word had come that the Germans were leaving Lamia. Down the tortuous mule track they came, through a landscape of sheer slopes and stunted trees, of small patches of cultivation, of boulders and thorny scrub. They passed through the short ruined street of Nea Yannitsou, nine kilometers on their way, and came to the remains of Platistomo, after four kilometers of similar road. Now there was only a short way to go before the main road was reached.

But Mulgan asked Tsoumas to guide him by paths that would avoid the main road, with its blackened villages and joyful populace. So they rode on into Lamia across cornfields and through olive groves, through vines and ploughed land, across farmyards and past ruined cottages. In *Report on Experience* Mulgan describes the rejoicing that met him on his ride to Lamia. "Along the road, through blackened villages, people came out to hang flowers on the mule saddles. They offered us drinks and sweet cakes . . ."

This may have happened to Mulgan in Lamia; on the ride, as Tsoumas testifies, he could not bring himself to face it. The guilt he felt at being the major factor contributing to the misery of the villagers in the Sperkheios Valley was too strong. The feeling finds expression in the concluding words of Chapter 9: "As we rode down, the last German trucks were still visible, winding up the road to Derven Fourka above Lamia. But victory had come to a tired and an old and a weary people. The road we travelled was lined with graves we could not see, and for each person that shook us by the hand we could imagine a son or a brother who should have been there to shelter us from reproach and was not there— being dead." [21]

After some days in Lamia, Mulgan had a sudden bout of malaria, which left him weak. He moved, in early November, to Athens. The city had been liberated for a fortnight, and ELAS had so far been unable to gain a footing in the capital, but the process was already beginning of infiltrating the city with *andartes* from the mountains; and the thorny question of restoring King George was still in the offing.

For a few days it was uncertain what the future of Force 133 personnel was to be. Then it was announced that the Allied Military Mission—and hence Force 133—was to disappear. As soon as he was fit Mulgan flew to Cairo, arriving on November 8. He took up residence at that houseboat on the Nile which served as headquarters for the members of the force in their comings and goings.

He wrote somberly and restrainedly to Gabrielle and his parents. To the former he wrote, regarding his future plans: "I've seen the New Zealanders who still live in Cairo and have applied for a transfer to the New Zealand army with the idea of coming out to New Zealand as soon as possible and then doing any further military service they may want from me from there. I don't think there will be any difficulty about this, but it may take a month or so to arrange, for the application has to go home to the War Office in England and then I'll have to wait for a boat." [22]

XI *Civilization Again*

Cairo was at first a relief. Mulgan wrote to his son Richard, now rising five, "I am really leading a very comfortable life, just waking up in the morning and ringing a bell for someone to bring me breakfast in bed. I don't know how I will get on when I come home since I will need a great many servants to look after me. However, perhaps you and Gabrielle will be able to manage between you." [23]

But the comforts of civilization, though relished keenly at first, soon began to pall. To Gabrielle he wrote, after only a fortnight in Egypt, "I don't get so much fun out of civilisation as I expected. The cleanliness and food are nice, but the entertainments are stale and unprofitable, and I find myself falling asleep after dinner every night." [24]

At the end of November Mulgan moved from the Force 133 houseboat to the Victoria Hotel, "a little quiet hotel in Cairo's main street."

He had begun again to write, but with some dissatisfaction found it difficult. "There has come to me more and more the conviction that I haven't very much to say and that only those who have a lot to say should write. On the other hand I think writing needs hard work like any other art, so I will keep on trying even if only as a hobby." [25]

When the Communist Revolution of December, 1944, broke out in Athens Mulgan was a dismayed though distant spectator. His instinctive sympathy with the ELAS troops he had fought with did not blind him to the ruthlessness and brutality of which the Communist leaders were capable. But the extreme British view, which condemned out of hand all left-wing organizations in Greece, seemed to him untenable. He laid a good deal of the blame on Churchill. "Those who have seen him recently say that he's very old and tired and dogmatic, not any longer able to listen to opinion and argument." [26]

Just before Christmas the Commander of Force 133 in Cairo— Colonel J. A. Dolbey—sent for Mulgan and asked him to take over the liquidation of SOE commitment in Greece. These are his words:

As I got to know John better since his return to Cairo, it became obvious to me that he was by far the best officer qualified for the job. Too many of our B.L.O's who had now come out of Greece lacked the objectivity and judgment required to investigate the record of the Greeks who had worked for our missions in order to recommend awards, to assess compensations in kind and in money, to set up scholarships for the orphans, hospital beds for the sick, etc., and ensure that the considerable sums that were finally paid out would not be eroded into dust in a short time by the devaluation of the drachma.[27]

Mulgan's answer was a refusal of the post. Dolbey was puzzled by this, since no serious reasons were given in explanation. Then several days later, just after Christmas, Mulgan came back to say that he would accept the job and go to Athens in command of what Dolbey had christened "Adv. Force 133."

The reason for his initial refusal was probably the expectation that either the New Zealand Division or the Oxford University Press would claim his services. A few days' reflection probably sufficed to show him that quick action from either of these quarters was most unlikely. In the letter announcing his decision to Gabrielle he simply says: ". . . feeling I couldn't wait indefinitely here, I've agreed to go back to Athens and help our own people there . . . It's sad and disappointing that I'm not coming home just yet and I resent the time and money I've wasted in Cairo, but the way the war has gone this winter I don't think there's anything to do about it and my release, which Sisam has asked for, isn't likely to come through until the European war has finished . . ."[28]

XII *Athens and Cairo*

He flew from Cairo in the early hours of the morning of January 14, woke to see the dawn coming up over Crete, and came down to an Athens that was a nightmare place—"broken windows, starving sad faces, and a smell of death and bad drainage."

Lou Northover, the tough sergeant who had been with him in the hills, was on his way back to New Zealand. So was Arthur Edmonds, of the original "Harling" party. He had no friends among the small group he found at 21A Amerikis Street, where the orderly room of Force 133 was situated, though Captain Michael Ward he knew from odd meetings in Thessaly.

A Greek girl who had worked as the secretary to the previous commanding officer remembers being taken into the room to meet her new boss. He was seated in a chair, occupied in unlacing his boots.

"Hang on a minute," he said glancing up with a grin, "till I get these boots off. They're killing me."

When he rose to greet her she saw a broad, powerful, bronzed figure, with fair wavy hair and a broad smile. His lack of self-consciousness did not deprive him of a natural dignity. They soon became close friends.

His job was a heartbreaking one.

I spend nearly all day in my office . . . and most of it is listening to sad tales in Greek . . . The situation of some of these people is so pitiful and there is so little at present that one can do for them. Many of them lost their husbands or sons working for us during the occupation and are now without food or work or help . . . It is the hell of a job. Nearly all this underground work was done without receipts or proper names being used and to try and dig out the truth of some incident that happened say three years ago is peculiarly difficult. Nor is it very amusing, though academically interesting, I suppose, to listen to people's stories of what happened to them in German prisons. They took a lot of our people that they had imprisoned for a long time and shot them just before they left Athens, sort of farewell gesture.[29]

Mulgan found Americans and British equally exasperating in their lack of understanding of the Greeks. The Americans championed the left-wing parties, ignoring the brutality which they had shown during the civil war. The British championed, just as one-sidedly, the right wing. "They are all loth to realize," he wrote, "that people in these countries are no longer normal."

The task of finding jobs and distributing food went on apace. He wrote back to Cairo, "It's very easy to place people with only a smattering of English. For others we can only find manual work at present, but that at least is something and a bigger variety of work will probably be available before we leave. At all events, these two things have produced a more cheerful atmosphere in our waiting rooms, since we can now do something concrete for people who come in, besides taking their particulars."

The murder by ELAS of those who had helped the British during the occupation was unfortunately a fact in many cases. In one letter to Cairo he says, "I saw Meyers last night . . . none of his stories was very pleasant . . . I'm afraid a fairly clean sweep has been made of our helpers in the mountain areas."

On March 15 he posted to Gabrielle the typescript of the book published as *Report on Experience.* With the manuscript came the following letter:

DEAREST GABRIELLE,

You asked me a long time ago to send you what I had been writing and I'm afraid I didn't. I'm sending you this now, in case I'm longer coming home than I hope, since I thought it might amuse you and perhaps you could type it for me. An odd little Greek typed the first part—he wanted to improve his English, though I doubt he took the best model for that. It isn't a book, but only the draft and outline of a book I'd like to write. I destroyed I'm afraid more than there is here and don't much like what there is but thought it best to finish off in outline and however short, the form of a book, since the habit of not writing grows on one. So I've written it down and if I had to publish it now, would call it "Summary of Experience," which is what it is. It has in it all the little that I've thought over this war and the peace that we're now coming to. It isn't as well said or as clearly written as it should be, and would need elaboration to be convincing. I think every man writes in the end just as much as he has in him to say, and I long ago realized that the little talent I have lacked inventiveness and wouldn't bear more than a certain strain being laid upon it. The fact that one has deep convictions about people and society and the way the world should be made to exist for us, doesn't mean that one can write a good book. What small virtues I have, some of them sadly cultivated with rather painful experience, are practical and don't lead to literature, or at least all the literature they've so far led to could be wrapped up in this small package I'm sending you now. However, I promise you sweetheart, if I ever do publish a book which I could be in any way proud of, I'll dedicate it to you—strictly against the rules we used to lay down for authors in the Press—as a slight gesture of thanks, and love, for all that you suffered from me in my younger and less sensible days.

I seem to be getting unnecessarily solemn and declamatory on this typewriter, it comes of writing late at night in the darkened city of Athens, so will just send you now my love—not in a dedication—and for Richard, the schoolboy, bless him,

JOHN

Mulgan finished up his job in Athens on April 15, and then took two days to go up into Euboea, where he had to see the families of some of those who were killed while assisting the English.

During his time in Athens, Mulgan's closest friendship was with his secretary, a Greek girl who spoke good English and had worked in the Bank of Greece. This girl saw a good deal of him. She says, "We became very friendly—often lunching and dining together. Colonel Mulgan, however, was a man of extreme reserve (at least that was my experience). Throughout his stay in Athens it was very obvious that he was depressed (we in Greece would describe him as 'melancholy') but whenever I asked him the reason—which I did on a number of occasions—he always changed the subject."

One of his brother officers says, "In the last month or so before he went down to Cairo and died there, he was keeping company a great deal with Zoi, who seemed to be his main companion and confidante at the time."

When Mulgan left for Cairo, Zoi asked him to keep in touch with her. He gave his quizzical grin and made a rather odd reply: "You will always know where I am in future."

XIII   *Death in Cairo*

Mulgan was back in Cairo on Thursday, April 19, and on the same day called on Dolbey. They had a brief talk about the termination of the business of dealing with Greek claims on Force 133, and on the next day Mulgan called again, when they had a long and detailed session that disposed of the bulk of the questions outstanding, though some loose ends still remained.

Dolbey states that Mulgan asked for leave to go to Alexandria for the weekend. He concurred, asking that Mulgan call on him at 9 A.M. on the following Wednesday, April 25. Almost certainly, the family Mulgan visited in Alexandria was that of his interpreter, Paul Contomichalos, who states, "I had seen him and talked to him just a few days before his death." [30]

Mulgan did not keep his 9 A.M. appointment with Dolbey on April 25, but came in at 6 P.M. that day. Dolbey was busy, and asked him to come back an hour later, which he did. They talked over the final list of questions that had to be settled and agreed to meet again next day at 9 A.M. On his way out, at about 7:30 P.M., Major Angus, the second-in-command of Force 133, reminded him of his appointment to go to Maadi the following day to see about his transfer to the New Zealand Army. Mulgan said he would come in and let him know how he got on.

Mulgan was staying at the Continental Hotel. A close friend of his, Mrs. Atherton, met Mulgan at 8 P.M.—after he had returned from Headquarters—in the corridor of the Continental Hotel, and he came to her room for a drink and a sandwich. He said he could not stay for dinner with her as he usually did, as he had an important business engagement at 9 P.M. A mutual friend who came to Mrs. Atherton's room took them both off to his room for another drink, but at 9 P.M. Mulgan left.

He went straight to his room on the third floor, where he was typing at 9:30 P.M., when he rang for a waiter, from whom he ordered a whiskey and soda and a packet of cigarettes. These were brought by an Egyptian, and at 10:30 P.M. the waiter who had answered his ring (and who was head waiter for the third floor) saw him leave the hotel. This man went off duty at 11 P.M. and the time at which Mulgan returned to his room is not known.

What he must have done was come back to his room, put on his pajamas, and open his medical kit, which still accompanied him. In it was a bottle with liquid morphia, and a tube of morphia tablets. He took all the morphia he had, went to sleep, and never woke up.

A housemaid looked in at 10 A.M. on the morning of April 26, saw Mulgan apparently asleep, and went away again. She looked in again twice during the day—at 12:30 P.M. and at 2:15 P.M., but thought he was still asleep.

When Mulgan did not keep his 9 A.M. appointment, Dolbey was not unduly worried. When 6 P.M. came and went, however, he thought he should find out where this officer was. He accordingly rang the Continental Hotel, and Mulgan's body was discovered.

In a letter which he left for Dolbey, Mulgan apologized for his suicide, and said he had reason to believe that he was suffering from cancer of the throat. He also asked Dolbey to suppress the fact of his suicide and to fabricate an account of an accident to explain his death.

There is no evidence that Mulgan had ever consulted a doctor over his throat (which was perfectly healthy). Dr. Robert Moyers of Iowa, who had been in the mountains with Mulgan, was emphatic that Mulgan would have mentioned any ailment to him, and that he never did.

Mulgan's suicide is an insoluble mystery: but Professor Nicholas Hammond, who saw much of him in Greece, is of the opinion that Mulgan should never have been sent back there in January. A year such as Mulgan had spent was, in his opinion, more than enough for the hardiest of men.[31]

CHAPTER 4

Journalism and Editing

MULGAN was always deprecating in his references to his own writing ability. Near the end of his life he wrote: "The fact that one has deep convictions about people and society and the way the world should be made to exist for us doesn't mean that one can write a good book." [1] In his early life, to the girl who was closest to him at Auckland University College, he confided that he would have liked to be a poet, but that he knew he could never surpass his father in that line. As we shall see, his judgment was correct. The impulse to write, which he acknowledges from time to time, he sees as a purely journalistic affair. Just a year after arriving in England he wrote to his father: "I think that if I had training as a journalist over here I could come back to a fairly good job in New Zealand." Two months later he repeats the remark: "With regard to my future . . . if it is possible I want to get into journalism because it seems a straight-forward career." [2]

How much the influence of his father's profession, how much that of his close friend Geoffrey Cox, was to be seen in these declarations it is hard to say. Certain it is that writing for publication was an activity that appealed to Mulgan from an early age. The account of his editorship of a third form magazine at Wellington College has been given elsewhere. A. E. Caddick, his formmaster at this time, comments on the high degree of critical sophistication the third-former possessed.

I *"Sea Fever"*

Two years later, when he was in the fifth form at the Auckland Grammar School, Mulgan had a short story accepted by an Auckland periodical, the *Weekly Press*. It was a full page narrative entitled "Sea Fever." For this he used a pen-name—"Arnold Freydon." The story is a highly romantic one, concerning a young skipper of a coastal scow, who has taken to a seafaring life as a result

74

of being crossed in love. On his first voyage he rescues a beautiful girl from a wrecked vessel, and is tempted to follow her back to city life. But the story ends as follows:

> He thought of the town, the dust and the smoke and the artificial life, and his mind was made up.
> "I'm sorry," he said, "but I'm born to the sea, and I can't leave it."
> They shook hands without another word, and he turned and went slowly up the gangway.

The story provides interesting testimony to two characteristics that Mulgan never lost—a love of the sea, and an impulse to write. The former gives authority and substance to the technical detail of "Sea Fever." Evidence for the latter is readily forthcoming. During his Auckland University College career, for instance, Mulgan became responsible for the official Students' Association publications—*Craccum* the newspaper, and *Kiwi* the literary annual. He also shared the responsibility for the Jubilee booklet which was published in 1933, the fiftieth anniversary of the foundation of the college.

II *Newspaper Articles*

After his arrival in England he wrote articles from time to time for the *Auckland Star*. These dealt with a variety of subjects: Oxford, London life, East Anglia, A. S. Neill's school at Summerhills, English farming—these were a few of the subjects treated. From the first Mulgan made it clear that he was interested in the unfamiliar facets of life which the English presented to him, but at the same time he retained an objective and dispassionate attitude very different from the uncritical adoration of all things English which, one gathers, had been usual in the New Zealand of his day. During the war he wrote to his wife: "When you consider that the ambition of every rich young girl in Auckland in my day was to be presented at Court you can understand that the society of the town is not likely to be highly desirable . . ." [3] And his early articles on Oxford ways were so censorious that his father, literary editor of the *Auckland Star*, refused to print them unless a more indulgent tone was adopted. These articles were written for the sake of the odd pounds they brought in, but Mulgan also manifested in them that questioning of commonly held values and assumptions that marked his whole life, from the time of the riots onward.

In addition to the articles he sent back, he was writing for himself. He projected a novel as early as August, 1936, when he wrote to his parents: "I'm working on a novel which I have about half done—I don't know how it will turn out, but I like doing it." [4] This novel was entitled "Journey to Oxford"; only a fragment of the typescript remains. It is clear that Mulgan was transmuting personal experience, using his writing as a means of distancing that experience, and of making judgments about the society to which, at Oxford, he had been introduced.

III *"Behind the Cables"*

But during 1936 he had another writing outlet which competed for his time and energy. This was the series (roughly three-weekly) of newsletters which he and Geoffrey Cox between them sent back to the *Auckland Star*. In order to produce the intelligent comment on current events which he wanted, Mulgan had to keep an attentive eye on a variety of periodicals. By this time the menace to the peace of Europe which fascism provided had made him anxious to interpret what was happening for the common reader. He never lost this wish to interest ordinary citizens in political processes. After the newsletter series had come to an end, he wrote to his father, at the beginning of 1938:

To people like myself—knowing that one isn't an artist of any kind— this seems like the time of the pamphlet and the article, where the importance . . . is . . . of persuading as many people as possible in the short time that's left which side they should be on.

Reading the newsletters thirty years after they were published convinces one of the competence of the team which was producing them, and of the seriousness with which the great events then taking shape were exhibited to the New Zealand reading public. Thus, though there is a good deal of trivia, every newsletter contains at least one mention of the international situation; most have more than one. For instance, on March 4, 1936, the chief items for comment are the opening of Parliament, the inquiry into arms manufactures, and the strike at Smithfield. Six weeks later, it is the meeting of the Council of the League of

Nations to consider the German occupation of the Rhineland. In September developments in the Spanish War occupy a part of every newsletter; in October the Nuremberg rally is the central item for comment.

The moderate tone and the readable style make the series impressive. It is no wonder that the editor of the *Auckland Star*, looking back, sees them as a landmark in the history of journalism in New Zealand.[5] The writing of *Man Alone* followed that of the newsletters. But before we turn to the novel, something may be said of the other writing which Mulgan was engaged on at this time.

IV   Poems of Freedom

The chief concern for 1937–38 was *Poems of Freedom,* begun in August, 1937 and published late in 1938. This work resulted from a half-serious suggestion offered by Mulgan to Victor Gollancz, early in 1937, that the Left Book Club audience which had grown up at that time would probably buy an anthology of poems which presented the theme of revolt against oppression. Gollancz agreed, stipulated that the title be *Poems of Freedom*—not "Poems of Revolt"—and commissioned Mulgan to proceed with the work.

Mulgan wrote to W. H. Auden inviting him to contribute a foreword, which Auden agreed to do. Mulgan then proceeded to select his poems and procure permissions to print those still under copyright. Unfortunately Gollancz allowed a very small sum for copyright fees, so that in the end, of the hundred and sixty-nine poems published, only just over thirty were modern. The bulk of the volume consists of nineteenth-century poems (ninety-four out of the hundred and sixty-nine); many of them rather empty rhetorical exercises. Still, there was a good deal of interesting material, and some of decided literary worth—like Yeats's "The Rose Tree," Whitman's "To a Foil'd European Revolutionary," several Blake poems, Morris's *The Voice of Toil,* and the extracts from *Piers Plowman.* The single Auden poem ("Brothers") is a poor one and there is a good deal too much indifferent Rex Warner. A single representative of New Zealand is included—R. A. K. Mason's "Youth at the Dance." Hugh Macdiarmid is represented by two poems. Auden's preface, light but serious, develops the theme of the poem as a register of common experience. "The primary function of poetry, as of all the arts, is to make us more aware of ourselves and the world around us."

Mulgan's editorial note is, in its way, more impressive than Auden's introduction. He writes with a sense of involvement that is lacking in Auden. The note begins directly and forcefully:

This anthology has been conceived in an effort to represent the liberalism of poetry in its oldest and widest sense. It would be unfair to the poets, both living and dead, whose work is represented here, to attempt to include them in any one political party. It would be as unfair to deny to them that just and generous belief which they all shared in the essential nobility of the human race—a nobility which causes men to go forward and when they can no longer go forward, to die.

Admitting that much of what is in the anthology is not good poetry, Mulgan claims it has relevance to the times, and he goes on:

Few of us in this post-war period have been unwilling either to work or to fight for the causes in which we believed. What we have witnessed has been the systematic destruction of a great many of those causes. But to those who think darkly of the future we could perhaps quote James Thomson's poem "Europe's Rouge-et-noir," which is included here. We could quote too, all those poems of the early nineteenth century, written at a time when a British government was playing a part in Europe as destructive of liberty and democracy as we see it playing today, and demonstrating just as clearly that axiom, that class is thicker than blood. That the consequences of such a policy are, in the modern period, fraught with infinitely greater possibilities of death and suffering for humanity, does not alter the certainty that the cause of "liberalism" will ultimately prevail.

These words demonstrate the seriousness with which Mulgan regarded the political situation. It is clear that he saw *Poems of Freedom* in much the same light as the newsletters—as a force in "persuading as many people as possible in the short time that's left what side they should be on."

V   The Emigrants

Seriousness, however, is not applicable to the work which was published soon after the anthology—the sketches of early travelers to the antipodes of which the final title was *The Emigrants*. To some extent this had been planned by Hector Bolitho with one eye on the approach of New Zealand's centennial year (1940). The volume is readable enough, though rather superficial. Where the "subjects" are allowed to speak for themselves, from journals and letters, interest remains high, but the linking narrative is not always free from clichés and baldness.

Mulgan was the author of the two most interesting sketches—those of Charles Armitage Brown and Charles Meryon. The latter traveled as a French naval officer to New Zealand in the 1840's. The study of Brown provided extracts from the then unpublished journal in the Keats Museum at Hampstead. Brown is an interesting figure because of his close association, when young, with Keats, and the story of his ill-fated venture to the new colony of New Zealand is an ironic contrast with the earlier literary life he led.

Hector Bolitho has this to say of his collaborator.:

His father, Alan Mulgan, helped me with my writing when I was on the staff of the *Star* in Auckland in 1919 and 1920. When John came to London, I helped him because of this. Instead of needing my help, it was soon apparent that he had every quality, of character and talent, to make him go his own way.[6]

VI *Mulgan's Verse*

During his undergraduate years Mulgan wrote poetry now and again, and had poems published in various New Zealand periodicals. These are all unremarkable; though technically quite skillful there is, in most of them, a conventional mistiness of feeling. Many are love-poems, slight, vague, and pretty, like this one:

Desideria

Just for the way her dark hair caught the light
or her gray eyes looked clearly,
or the touch of her hand as we parted, saying goodnight?
Was it for this merely?
Or her voice, sweet and quiet
or the lithe, swift turn of her head?
Was it for this that I loved her so dearly
and then no more?
Though I grow old and weary
and my days are full of night

> I shall not know
> why I first loved her in the long ago
> and loved her so dearly.

Even so, it is worth noting that there is a quality of baffled questioning in the poem which is at variance with the lyric tone, the gracefully conventional melancholy, and the flat diction. Mulgan's honest mind can be detected at work, even though he clearly lacks the poet's instinct for language.

There is one poem, however, which is of more than passing interest. This is "Old Wars," written during his final year at Merton, in 1935. It is interesting in that it provides evidence that the theme of *Man Alone* was long meditated. The text of the poem, never published, and existing only in typescript among Mulgan's papers, is as follows:

Old Wars

Thinking there would be war again
I said to Johnson, old-timer,
sitting in the sun half sleeping
Tell me of the war that you fought in,
tell me of the long campaigning
in Suvla, Lemnos and Passchendaele,
and of the retreat from St. Quentin to Amiens.
And he laughed then, mournfully not merrily.
In the young sunlight were the trees black-standing
that burned long years ago and never fell,
and at his feet the old dog sleepily
stirred as he laughed.
Tell me of the war-days, I asked him,
Not of the camps and laughter that I know,
but tell me of the trenches and the fighting
and the men you killed when you were young.

And we went out through the fields into the sunlight
and over hills of fern,
and the old dog came, sleepily following.
In the dark paddock by the pine trees
was grass, green, heavy with richness
until we came to the wide sheep valleys
where the ewes strayed eagerly questing
by black logs fallen and harsh.

There'll be no war, said Johnson, no need
for talking of the days when I was young:
I am grown old, he said, no more the fighting
nor the long march and fever of recall.
And we came to a small river that lingered
on stones beneath the fern.
There are trout there, he said, for I remember
days as a boy beside that quiet pool.
And we crossed on the stones stepping carefully,
but the old dog stood long in the water
broke thirst and rejoiced in its coolness.
It is long now, said Johnson, remembering
the bush we cleared and burned,
the rata, rimu and black matai,
and men are dead that long since laboured here.
There'll be no war, said Johnson, more urgent,
no need for travelling beyond the seas
and dim enough are all the days of fighting
that came upon the years when I was young.

And we turned then and silent went westward,
away from the sun,
and silent we came to the homestead
low down in the pines.

In 1935, when this poem was written, fascism had established itself as a threat to Europe, and Mulgan was uneasily becoming aware that war was far from unthinkable. The interesting point is that he returns to dwell on the landscape of New Zealand—the ravaged landscape of fallen trees, the hot sun, the trout stream. He is emotionally involved with the country; and he associates it with conflict.

Here then is the genesis of *Man Alone*, even to the appearance of Johnson, the veteran of World War I. The involvement will be dissipated by the writing of the novel. After *Man Alone*, Mulgan is free to attend wholeheartedly to the tragedy of Europe.

CHAPTER 5

Why Fiction? Origins of an Impulse

WHEN one studies the writing Mulgan had done up to the time when he began *Man Alone,* that novel seems an incongruous interpolation. Journalistic impressions of England's countryside and customs; factual essays on early pioneers in New Zealand; explanatory journalistic footnotes to the political scene, English and European; condensations of literary reference works; a collection of poems on the common theme of political liberty; popular lectures on politics for the Workers' Educational Association: these were the enterprises which, as we have seen, engrossed Mulgan during the three years immediately preceding the composition of *Man Alone.* The last four were still occupying his attention, in the time he could spare to them from the all-absorbing activity of learning a new and exacting job in the secretariat of a great publishing house. Yet these enterprises were all abruptly interrupted, during the winter of 1937–38, the first winter of Mulgan's marriage. Between December and April he wrote the sixty thousand words which comprise Part I of *Man Alone.*

The manner in which he wrote is also, in its way, revealing. To his young wife he said almost nothing of what he was doing. He had so many projects afoot that she was not curious. Besides, she knew all about the condensation of the *Oxford Companion*—she was doing a good deal of the mechanical work involved; about the "Behind the Cables" series she also knew a good deal, since Mulgan's method of writing these was to sit down as soon as he came in from a visit to London, with the *Times* and the *Daily Worker* beside him, and compose his column on the typewriter while he had a drink before the evening meal. The W.E.A. lectures, too, held no secrets for her, since she had sat in the audience for a number of them. Yet it was not until the novel was completed that she knew her husband had been working on fiction. She knew he had been writing something about New Zealand, for she had seen him poring over a large map of the North Island. The composition of the book, however, as far as she was concerned, took place behind a veil of secrecy.

One may ask why Mulgan was impelled to write what is, on the face of it, an adventure story at this point of his career. *Man Alone* ultimately appeared along with other popular novels on the list of a small publisher whose speciality was light fiction. Once the book was published Mulgan forgot it—at all events, he makes only a single ironic and jesting reference to it in his subsequent correspondence. He did not think of himself as a novelist. His real interest—and it was a passionate and abiding one—was in the problem of reconciling effective government with social justice. Why, then, did he drive himself to this single compulsive sweep of literary creation?

I *Pressures from the Past*

The answer to this question is to be found in the beginnings of Mulgan's life in New Zealand, in his family background, and in the qualities of his own character.

The principal fact which is relevant to Mulgan's departure from New Zealand was that he had been rejected. However it had happened, the Rhodes Scholarship which, as every sane person who knew the facts would agree, he well deserved, had been withheld from him. More, this miscarriage of justice appeared to derive from Mulgan's outspoken espousal of the cause of free speech and social justice. A provincial society had revenged itself on an intellect more keen and a vision more clear than was customary: intellect and vision were permissible, providing they were trained on neutral subjects. To query the assumptions by which the New Zealand establishment in mid-Depression guided the country elicited a strong countermovement. The ironic fact is that three years later the whole outlook had changed: the battle had been fought and won. But Mulgan left when it seemed that New Zealand was locked in a frozen Antarctic of conventional and reactionary obscurantism.

The dissatisfaction Mulgan felt with the society which could tolerate with complacence the miseries of the unemployed was increased when, after arriving in England, he had to see through the press his father's two books—the novel *Spur of Morning*, and the travel book *A Pilgrim's Way in New Zealand*. The first-

named was the object of several visits which Mulgan paid to publishers in London in the winter of 1933–34. He tried Longmans,
Hodder and Stoughton, and Heinemann, among others, before he
succeeded in placing the book with Dent. He wrote to his father
announcing this news on May 4, 1934.

Mulgan's attitude to his father was a complex one, and is perhaps worth trying to understand. Superficially, they were the best
of friends, which is not surprising, for Alan Mulgan was a thoroughly good-natured and lovable man whose friends in all walks
of life were multitudinous. On the other hand, this very quality of
outgoing benevolence was a handicap to the family as a whole,
for it meant that the father spent little time with his children—
much less than the average New Zealand parent. To one girl in
Auckland Mulgan made the remark that his father "never brought
him up."

Nevertheless, as one can see from the admiring tone of the
letters to his father from Wellington College, Mulgan was very
sensible of the latter's literary standing, and he had a genuine
admiration for some of his verse. Yet as he grew up he became
aware of the thinness of his father's literary equipment. The
weekly essays which Alan Mulgan published in the *Auckland Star*
under the nom de plume of "Cyrano" were interesting enough and
cleverly enough written to absorb the average non-literary reader
—light essays in the manner of J. C. Squire and the *London Mer-
cury*, of the middle-brow cheerfulness of *John O'London's
Weekly*. In other words, with a wealth of elegant allusiveness, and
a tone of well-read urbanity, they said next to nothing.

II   Home

Alan Mulgan's greatest literary success had been the travel
book which he wrote after his return from a journey to England in
1925–26. Entitled *Home: A Colonial's Adventure*,[1] the book went
very quickly through three editions. In it, the writer gives an
ecstatic account of the country he had set out to find—the dream
of cosiness, antiquity, and security with which the pioneer had
comforted himself in the wilderness. Alan Mulgan met a number
of literary figures in London, but the one he set most store by was
his hero J. C. Squire. The picture he paints of twentieth century
England was limited, sentimental, and conventional in the extreme.

What his son came to think of it is to be found in Chapter Two of *Report on Experience,* where he says:

We can dispense now with the legend which tradition fostered for us of a benign England, the staid old mother of the seven seas. I don't know whether this England of our story books ever existed. It was a country, as I remember it, of rounded, lovely hills, its slate-roofed villages rich in history. In this faery England the aristocracy were patriarchal and humane. Men worked on the land for love as well as profit, and played cricket in the long summer evenings. Rose-cheeked children went happily to the village school.[2]

This might be a summary account of the atmosphere of *Home.* When he reached England Mulgan became forcibly aware of the falsity of his father's picture, for he goes on:

No-one told us that in England the villages had died, that farming had ceased to be an occupation for men and had become an expensive hobby for gentlemen. None of the books explained that in England men spoke different languages, that the well-to-do had given up the accents of their counties and adopted the accents of a class.

England was Tilbury on a raw November morning, streets of tenement houses crowded with pale, flat-capped working men who obviously had no work. England was wide-ribboned roads littered with facile, emotionless suburbs, a countryside ravaged by charabanc parties, old buildings and memorials commercialized into quaintness.

III Spur of Morning

The bitter tone of this passage must convey something of the profound disappointment which the real face of Britain aroused in him. More immediately he perceived the superficiality of his father's writing, and when he had to take the manuscript of *Spur of Morning* round to publishing houses he became well acquainted with the unsatisfactory nature of that piece of writing too. *Spur of Morning* is a conventionally planned novel of life in Auckland in the early years of the twentieth century and is based on Alan Mulgan's own memories of that time. There is some merit in the reporting of life and manners, and there are some lively pieces of action prose—an account of a rugby football match, for example. But by and large the book is as superficial, in its way, as *Home* had been.

Spur of Morning thus rests upon complacently held assumptions which the author has never examined or challenged. His son picked this up straightaway, and though he never ventured on a degree of outspokenness that would have hurt his father, he did remonstrate. In June, 1934 he told his father with a casualness no doubt intended to disguise the enormity of what he was doing, that he had rewritten some parts.

I cut out one sentence in which you said that one would always find the Trent household the same "perhaps a little mellower"—but I am struck by the difference of our points of view. I can feel your sincerity when you write, but as a modern I would say that it isn't true as a description of life. What I mean is that people don't marry and live happily ever after, that life isn't just falling in love with someone and everything is all right, it's a succession of little incidents and worries and reactions. When one looks at a nice bit of coastline one can't isolate everything and just have the reaction from it—one thinks about having a cup of tea, or the person one is with, or something in the past or future, and only very rarely and usually in recollection does it come back at all vividly. I think that if you have believed in these things they have been true for you, but my generation can't accept them any longer. I think we are without standards. No-one I meet here believes in anything. But the answer I think is to be sincere in one's reactions and emotions and just live as living and see what happens.

His father did not accept such cavalier treatment of his manuscript without demur. He wrote somewhat testily to his son; but in October the latter replied, a shade less courteously, but just as imperturbably:

Re the omissions, I still don't think they matter. I am afraid I found your fisherman dull. As for obstetrics, I did cut out a phrase about "the bloom of approaching motherhood," which haunts me still, and to say baldly that Barbara was going to have a baby seems unnecessary —even in this age—it's not as if her pregnancy matters a damn.

The directness of this criticism is tempered at the close of the letter, when Mulgan says (not altogether sincerely, one feels): "I feel like Pope editing Shakespear." Later in the year Alan Mulgan, indefatigably pursuing publication, sounded his son on the possibility of publishing some of his "Cyrano" articles as a collection of essays. One senses the way his son quails at the thought in the definiteness of his reply: "I don't think I should send the Cyrano articles home, at least not entirely as they are . . . You have your New Zealand reputation 'aere perennius'—I should think of Gerald Gould, and home reviewers."

It is certain that Mulgan was highly embarrassed by his father's novel. He thought it a slight book. This opinion was quite unequivocally expressed later to his wife. But he was too kindhearted to give his father a brutally frank opinion. If someone was willing to publish *Spur of Morning*, then he would not injure its reputation by speaking against it. Nevertheless, he must have writhed inwardly from time to time, as he contemplated the sentimental and untrue picture of life in New Zealand which that book offered the reader.

The relief with which he finds something to set against the superficiality of *Spur of Morning* is evident a couple of months later, when he writes to his father his opinion of Robin Hyde's volume of reminiscences, *Journalese*. Robin Hyde was the pen-name of Iris Wilkinson, a girl who had worked on various newspapers in New Zealand, and who was later to make a reputation as a novelist and poet. In *Journalese* she reports faithfully yet amusingly the experiences she has had as a reporter. Mulgan was touched by the book. "It *is* 'journalese,'" he wrote to his father, "and impressionism and badly written, but I have seen nothing else which describes the indeterminateness of life in a New Zealand city so well. It was really painful to read—what a life she has led—with a lot of cheapjacks and crudity and with poetry coming out of it all the time."[3] Perhaps Alan Mulgan felt a twinge of unease at this praise of a book which he must have despised for its lack of elegance and urbanity. It could hardly be lost on him that these words had been penned at the very time when the manuscript of his own book—*A Pilgrim's Way in New Zealand*[4]—was in John's possession and was being discussed with the Oxford University Press.

IV A Pilgrim's Way

This second piece of literary agency work which Mulgan did for his father was perhaps even more embarrassing to him than the first. The commissioning of *A Pilgrim's Way in New Zealand* was due to the success of *Home*. Alan Mulgan was now to do for

his own country what he had so felicitously performed for England
—body forth, through his own personal testimony, the common-
place stereotype which the average man harbored in his breast.
This stereotype was that of the scenic wonderland—the majestic
peaks of Switzerland, the thermal pools and geysers of Iceland,
the sub-tropical forests, the beaches and coastline of the South
Seas, the smiling pastureland of England, the fiords of Norway—
all contained in the two islands of New Zealand. The inhabitants
of this country, however, were of a single kind—they were true
blue Britishers to a man (if one excepted their Maori neighbors,
who were as true blue as their dark skins allowed them to be).
When he realized that this was the image of New Zealand that his
father was preparing to project, Mulgan wrote despairingly
home:

> The trouble is that Parnwell and Sisam, who has read it, don't know
> anything about New Zealand—what they want is tourist New Zealand
> —they like all the photos of mountains, but not those of towns . . .
> They don't want New Zealand represented as it is. I am disappointed
> that they should want that kind of book. It bears out, however, my
> former feeling that you could write something of what you feel about
> New Zealand that would be literature and needn't fulfil any guide-
> book pretensions.[5]

He overrated his father's ability. A *Pilgrim's Way* may have
been written to a formula but it is even so an excruciating book—
arch, pompous, spuriously lyrical by turns. Annoyingly, Alan Mulgan takes an imaginary tour round New Zealand with an imaginary Englishman, to whom he displays his country, and whose
reactions he tries to foresee. "Your eye will dwell on the farm-
houses. Some of them look like homes; some do not . . ." In the
bush: "You must be wary what leaves you grasp, for some are
knife edged . . ." Of town life: ". . . You may walk about a New
Zealand city for a week and never see a frock coat or top
hat . . ."

This grotesquely patronizing tone is matched by the disastrous
foreword, written by none other than Viscount Bledisloe, then
Governor-General of New Zealand. Doubtless Alan Mulgan congratulated himself on having secured a name to introduce his
book to the public. But at what a cost! There can have been few

more turgid or pretentious forewords ever written. Here is a random sample:

He [Alan Mulgan] displays within these pages not merely the ripened fruits of historical and topical research, presented with a lightness of touch which defies boredom, but a wealth of poetical afflatus and a capacity for word-painting which make perusal of his book a source of intellectual and spiritual refreshment.

The dust-jacket was as unfortunate as the foreword. The designer hit on the device, advanced for 1935, of photo-montage. But the three photos chosen are equally unexciting. A 1925 Dodge tourer on a bush road appears to be in a state of levitation over the heads of a flock of crossbred sheep which in their turn seem about to stream up the front steps of the Auckland War Memorial Museum.

An indication of Mulgan's embarrassment is the fact that *A Pilgrim's Way in New Zealand* was a book he never showed his wife—nor did he even refer to it. She was totally unaware of its existence, until well after her husband's death.

V   *The South Seas Seen from the North*

By the time *A Pilgrim's Way in New Zealand* was safely through the press, Mulgan had got his First, had begun work under Kenneth Sisam at the Clarendon Press in Walton Street, and in his spare time was working for Hector Bolitho on the sketches of early emigrants to New Zealand. Through these various activities his vision of New Zealand was being brought more and more into focus. His work at the Clarendon Press, for instance, brought him into contact with some of the most learned men in England, whom he found, for the most part, unassuming men of great integrity. When he compared them with visitors from New Zealand the contrast was glaring. Of one friend who came in August, 1935, he wrote:

I wish these women wouldn't be so consciously intellectual when they arrive in England. The last thing I want to do is talk about T. S. Eliot at breakfast, and as for the beauties of Oxford . . . I don't mind looking at them but I will not talk about them . . . New Zealand people seem to lack poise . . .

On the other hand he did, as Bolitho put it in the foreword to *The Emigrants* ". . . care deeply for New Zealand." Mulgan's first year in England was marked by acute homesickness. "To speak truly," he says himself, "all that I can really call to mind of those first few weeks at Oxford is the fire that I used to stare at, while I thought of other things, of sun and sea and summer coming to all the people I knew on the other side of the world." [6]

During the subsequent two years Mulgan was to harbor his memories of New Zealand—physical memories of the light and the form of the landscape; of personalities and happenings; of harshness and beauty, softness and grandeur, in the land itself; of callous and cheerful indifference, unprincipled meanness and pettiness, hard-hearted cupidity in the people of the land. "It's an odd country," he wrote to his mother in May 1936, "I feel very attached to it and yet very critical."

The appeal to his father to write out of the fullness of his experience and tell the whole truth about New Zealand had fallen on deaf ears. His own career, it appeared, was going to link his fortunes permanently with Britain, a contingency he tacitly assented to by marrying an English girl in mid-1937, and preparing to settle down in England. At the same time, every winter he felt like a physical pain the grey sunlessness of the English winter, considered what it would mean to return to the antipodes, and wondered whether he could do so with any satisfaction. "Old Wars," as we have seen, is evidence of such a feeling. It may have been the acute illness he underwent in the middle of the first winter of his marriage that turned his thoughts to the writing of a novel of New Zealand life. The unaccustomed leisure which his convalescence entailed gave him a unique occasion to review and order his feelings. The gestation and birth of *Man Alone* is obscure, but one can feel reasonably sure that this is what happened, for he began writing as soon as he returned home to Oxford.

So, in implied disagreement with his father's optimistic complacency, in bitter recognition of the remorseless malice of New Zealand society towards himself, the book was begun, and completed by April. Mulgan was hoping, by this act of creation, to exorcise the spirit of nostalgia which still haunted him. His statement in *Report on Experience* makes this clear.

I came in the end to know that . . . the land and the people whom we know when we are young stay with us and haunt us until we die . . . If you try to fight against this truth, and forget the country of your youth as I did for a long time, you will lose the fight and wither internally of homesickness.[7]

He would distance his homeland by writing objectively about it; recreate its essential nature, and so lay the ghost of his memories and turn his mind to the country he had adopted.

When the first draft was completed, he could write with satisfaction to his father: "I don't think I want to write, except perhaps as a journalist to describe something one sees, or later in my life. I haven't written or wanted to write any poetry for three years." [8] Though *Man Alone* is not mentioned, it would appear that these words were prompted by the exhaustion consequent on the effort of writing the first draft of the novel. The mention of poetry also has its interest, for the last poem Mulgan had written (in March, 1935) was the one entitled "Old Wars" which can be regarded as the starting point of *Man Alone*.

VI *Original Title*

The justification of this assertion may be seen in one detail. When he was writing this first draft of the novel, Mulgan had adopted a working title which his publisher found unserviceable and obscure. It was "Talking of War." This is indeed an odd title to apply to the story Mulgan wrote, but if one briefly considers the times in which he was writing one explanation may be that the title mirrors his own feeling of the moment. In February, 1938, when he was well on with the book, he wrote despondently on the turn affairs had taken in Europe.[9] The trend of events seemed clear enough: there was nothing to talk of now except war. The true significance of this first title becomes apparent when the book is critically examined. But first let us follow the vicissitudes of the first draft, "Talking of War."

Mulgan put his manuscript in the hands of a literary agent, and turned back with relief to the multifarious tasks that were awaiting his attention. His agent had no success, and Mulgan heard little from him during the summer and autumn of 1938. Early in the new year, however, he contacted the agent once more and urged a renewed effort to place the book. The result was that in March, 1939 Henry Kerby, the managing director of Selwyn and

Blount, a small publishing firm in London, wrote to Mulgan and stated his firm's willingness to publish the book. He made one stipulation, which a quotation from his letter will make clear:

There is one point, however. I will not be able to do it at its present length. Can you see your way to tacking on an extra twenty to twenty-five thousand words—in fact, to bring it up to eighty thousand? All my readers are unanimous in saying that with your probable fund of Spanish adventures this will present no difficulty. If you could see your way to doing this, I should like the completed MS by the end of June.[10]

VII   *The Writing of Part II*

This was an exasperating turn of events. By now Mulgan was waiting for war to come, and also seriously considering the possibility of a move to join the *Winnipeg Free Press*. Yet once again he pushed aside his preoccupations and sat down to the job of supplying Henry Kerby with his extra twenty thousand words of story. It is a measure of his literary good sense that he turned a deaf ear to Kerby's suggestions, eschewed any adventures in Spain, and devoted himself to providing a companion picture to that of Part I where farm life in New Zealand figures largely. In Part II he draws on his own experience of farm life in Britain, and follows Johnson's fortunes, with satisfying consistency, until he leaves him in the Spanish War.

The preoccupation uppermost in Mulgan's mind in Part II of the novel is the coming European struggle—then only three months away. And he gave Kerby very much less than he asked for—six thousand words instead of twenty thousand. Kerby accepted with equanimity this rather perfunctory gesture of acquiescence on Mulgan's part, but he stood out for a change of title, sending three possibilities to choose from:

1. "A Man Alone"
2. "Escape from Death"
3. "Living Space"

Mulgan chose the first, with the omission of the article. But it was not his title. The agreement embodies his working title—"Talking of War."

CHAPTER 6

"Something Nobody Counted On" [1]

*M*AN ALONE bears the stamp of Hemingway's influence. Mulgan was undoubtedly an admirer of the American writer (his letters have several affectionate references to "Ern Hem"); but he did not blindly imitate him. Rather, he borrows Hemingway's attitude to experience, his cool detachment, and his spare style of narration. Yet Mulgan's prose has its own inner structures and rhythms, which are wholly unlike Hemingway's.

I *The Plot of* Man Alone

The story of *Man Alone* is of the simplest, yet it is presented with a deceptive ease which conceals a quite high degree of sophistication. The story concerns Johnson, an immigrant to New Zealand in 1919, but Johnson is at the same time actualized and distanced by Mulgan's narrative scheme. The nameless narrator of the story encounters Johnson in Brittany, on leave from the war in Spain. The narrator would like to talk about the fighting, but Johnson will not talk about it—nor about the Great War, in which he had fought.

"I couldn't tell you about the war," Johnson said. "It wasn't a lot different from anything else. I could tell you worse things about the peace."
"What was the peace?"
"That was the bit in between."
"Worse things?"
"Truer things."
And so I said to him, not wanting to move and quite ready to listen: "Tell me about the peace then."

So Johnson's story is told, not in the first person, but detachedly by the anonymous narrator. Johnson lands in New Zealand, hopeful of making a good life in a new country, in 1919. He is willing

to work, and he does work. He gets a job on a farm in the Waikato (south of Auckland), then is tempted to join another returned soldier on a poor farm in the hills to the west of the Waikato Valley. But this venture ends when he perceives that the
farm is too poor to support more than its owner. So Johnson goes
off to Northland where he spends a lazy period on the swag, before he is signed on as deckhand on a coastal scow. This life he
finds very much to his taste and he would probably have remained in it, but the ship ceases its run and Johnson is paid off.

The time of the Economic Depression has now arrived, and
Johnson can obtain only a series of casual jobs. Even those become harder to get, until finally he ends up in a relief camp for
the unemployed, situated in the Waitakere Ranges, northwest of
the city of Auckland. Johnson marches with his fellow workers to
a mass meeting which is being held in the Auckland Town Hall.
The workers are prevented by the police from entering the hall, a
scuffle begins, spreads, and becomes a riot, in which shop windows are broken and looting occurs. Johnson sees his friend Scotty
being beaten by a police sergeant, intervenes, and as a result of
attacking the sergeant becomes himself the object of police pursuit.

He escapes, stows away on a goods train, and lands up in the
King Country, where he manages to get a job working on a remote
farm for the reserved and crude Stenning, whom he respects for
his qualities of doggedness and endurance. Stenning's half-caste
wife Rua becomes fond of Johnson, and he begins a rather half-
hearted affair with her. Unfortunately Stenning senses what is
happening, his attitude to Johnson changes, and Johnson decides
it is time he moved on again. The night before he is due to leave,
however, Rua comes to his sleeping hut and announces that she is
leaving with him in the morning. She has hardly told Johnson this
unwelcome news when Stenning's voice is heard outside, summon-
ing Johnson out. Johnson knows he is carrying the shotgun which
always accompanies his nocturnal walks. Rua has blown out the
candle he lit, and had locked his door when she came into his hut.
Stenning, a jealous husband, has to all appearances caught his
farmhand *in flagrante delicto* with his wife. He breaks in the
door, and Johnson closes with him, attempting to wrest the gun
from his grasp. But it goes off, killing Stenning.

As a result of this, Rua becomes panic-stricken and makes her escape back to the village where her people live, some miles away. Johnson, realizing that she is likely to misrepresent what has happened, decides to take to the bush. He hastily packs a swag and rides away in the direction of the wild hill country to the east— the rugged and unpeopled Kaimanawa Ranges. He remains several months in hiding. Then, when he thinks the hue and cry may have died down, and when he realizes that before long he will be too weak to move, he continues his journey, arriving by a fortunate stroke of luck at the hut of an old eccentric named Bill Crawley, who looks after him until the spring.

At length Johnson cautiously makes his way down into Hawkes Bay, and gets back to Hamilton, the center of the Waikato, where bad luck brings him face to face with Rua. He scares her into temporary silence, but realizes it is imperative to leave the country if he can. So he contacts the skipper of the scow he had worked on (who has now retired) with the idea of enlisting his help to obtain a secret passage on a boat leaving for overseas. Petersen, the old captain, is far from approving of Johnson's deeds, but complies with his request out of regard for past friendship. Johnson is smuggled aboard an oil tanker, and Part I concludes with his surveying the New Zealand coast as it falls astern in the setting sun.

In Part II Johnson's fortunes in England are pursued. He works on a large farm in Northamptonshire, and saves his money to pay back his brother (who had lent him the money to get out of New Zealand). The Spanish Civil War breaks out just when his timid brother is suffering a paroxysm of panic through a stranger's having come to inquire whether anything had been heard of Johnson. The brother agrees to forgo the balance of the loan if Johnson will leave the country. Johnson agrees, leaves the farm, and settles temporarily in London, working in a garage washing cars. He becomes friendly with an Irishman, O'Reilly, and when the latter goes to join the International Brigade in Spain, Johnson goes with him. In the brief epilogue the anonymous narrator relates that Johnson came through several battles, was wounded once in the arm, but was with the International Brigade when it was evacuated from Spain. Thus, though at the end of the book Johnson's whereabouts is unknown, he is still alive.

II *The Fortunes of* Man Alone

When the book was published, it was greeted with a mixture of
bewilderment and incomprehension. Most critics took Part II to
be the key to the whole work—for which they might be forgiven,
since in its laconic way it gives perspective to Part I, and seems to
lead Johnson out into a broader prospect of world political move-
ments. When Mulgan's wife went to New Zealand in 1941, her
mother-in-law went to some lengths to convince her that New
Zealand was not as *Man Alone* painted it to be.

The outbreak of war in September, 1939 caused the novel to
recede with rapidity into an oblivion that its author assumed to be
permanent. "Poor old Johnson," he wrote in 1942, ". . . like beer
without alcohol." How many copies were sold no one can tell, for
Selwyn and Blount lost all their stock and their records in the
London blitz of 1940. In 1949, however, New Zealand's most
enterprising publisher, Blackwood Paul (who had known Mulgan), undertook a new edition of the book. It sold out over the
succeeding ten years with a steadiness that inspired the confidence to undertake a further reprinting in 1960. This sold out in
half the time the previous edition had taken, and a further reprinting came out in 1965. The book has become something of a standard work in the post-primary reading lists of New Zealand.
Teachers find that fifth-formers read it with avidity, on the adventure story level. It has appeared as a set work in the English program of one university.

Much of the dissatisfaction felt by early readers of the book
originated in the character of the central figure. John C. Reid in
his *Creative Writing in New Zealand* was probably voicing the
commonly-held current opinion when he objected to the flatness
of Johnson's character and saw in it a pastiche of Hemingway's
"dumb ox" heroes. It is indeed this criticism of his own creation
which Mulgan himself made in 1943. "Beer without alcohol"—
Johnson, in other words, is not himself a particularly exciting or
compelling creation.

III *Character of Johnson*

Mulgan goes out of his way, in fact, to create a figure the re-
verse of heroic—a nondescript twentieth-century Everyman,
whose ordinariness is from the beginning insisted upon.

. . . a medium-sized man, very brown, almost black from the sun, with a round, ordinary-looking face and a large mouth and strong teeth stained yellow with tobacco. He had fair hair and no hat and eyes that were either grey or green . . .

There is, in fact, nothing much to individualize Johnson. He is docile, hardworking, friendly. He comes out to New Zealand in search of the country he has heard New Zealanders talk about in England. "The way they talked about it made it seem like the only country in the world."

What is Mulgan's purpose in making such a nonentity the center of his book? The answer, if we remember the circumstances prompting him to write, is clear. He is interested not in personality but in social process. Not Johnson, but the life Johnson encounters, is the real subject of the book. Hence the essential soundness of Johnson's personality for the purposes of the novel. A representative of an older civilization; not a thinker, but tried by adversity so that he has a kind of rough wisdom; a companionable man but one with resources of his own: Johnson is a good type of reflecting mirror in which the quality and texture of New Zealand life can be seen for what it is.

That life was seen by Mulgan in a quite specific light. It is at this point that we should recall his working title—"Talking of War," which covered Part I. This title, for a narrative which deals with life in New Zealand between 1919 and 1932, is a clear statement of purpose. Mulgan is going to show that life in New Zealand during the peace—"the bit in between"—is a struggle in its way as ferocious as the physical struggle involved in warfare. He is, in fact, giving an oblique answer to his father, to *Spur of Morning* and *A Pilgrim's Way in New Zealand.* (The latter title might have served, in a bitterly ironic way, for *Man Alone.*) "Here is New Zealand," Mulgan might be saying, "a very different place from the cardboard Edwardian maisonette of *Spur of Morning,* and from the technicolor poster jungle of *A Pilgrim's Way;* much closer, in fact, to the chaotic and untidy crudities of Robin Hyde's *Journalese.*" So he makes his central character register the land, the people; work, play; politics, love.

IV   A Shortage of Love

If we take the last quality first we shall deal with it very briefly.
Love is virtually non-existent in *Man Alone*. Johnson makes physical love with Rua contentedly enough, but his emotions are hardly
involved. He sees her, before long, as a vague danger. "He felt
himself sick with her and with what they were doing . . . [Rua]
did not matter to him at all." [2] The only other approaches to
women that Johnson embarks upon are with the melancholy tart
in Auckland on the night of his arrival, and with Mabel—"Mabel
at twenty-three, strong, solid, and wanting a husband." [3]

It is in Johnson's relations with Mabel that we discover a constantly recurring theme in the pattern of New Zealand life—the
economic theme. Johnson is interested enough in Mabel to walk
out with her, to kiss her in the back of the car at dances. But
Mabel's father interposes. "Mabel's father had ideas about buying
a farm." [4] He reads Johnson a lecture on how to acquire land:

You get a good team of horses and hire them out and work around
with them. You make money that way. You want to get half-cleared
land and bush land and clear it. That's what you want to do. The
missis and I chopped firewood outside the back door when we moved
in here. [5]

Mabel's father has interposed between his daughter and Johnson
the predominant fact of life in New Zealand: that normal human
relationships must give way to considerations of money: and that
these considerations go back, in one way or another, to the struggle to wrest a living from the inhospitable land. In other words,
Mulgan sees the whole fabric of human existence pulled barbar-
ously awry, by the war men fight against their adversary—the
country itself.

The pity of it is that the dream which brought the first settlers
to the South Seas was a dream of human perfectibility: the per-
plexities and corruptions of Europe were to be left behind; the
best preserved and improved, the worst forgotten. The dream
finds expression even as early as the 1820's when Dumont D'Ur-
ville, cruising round the shores of New Zealand, saw in its uninhabited spaces the promise of an ideal civilization. He wrote: [6]

The coast, which . . . had been lofty and mountainous, drops after Tokomaru Bay and slopes gently down to the sea. The surrounding country offers to the gaze of the navigator smiling woods, lovely valleys and two or three *pas*[7] of some considerable size. One of them, especially, situated about a league from the sea, a white patch in the middle of a space cleared of trees, with its regular lines of huts forming an amphitheatre reminded me somewhat of the little towns in the Greek Archipelago. This spontaneous comparison of the cradle of the highest European Civilization with these wild shores, induced in my mind a flood of reflections on the destinies of peoples . . .

V *Deficiency Sickness*

It is, in fact, the last falsified mutations of this dream that Mulgan is answering—those mutations found in his father's books. He is opposing to them the observed reality. Johnson has arrived in the country seeking the dream—"the way they talked about it made it seem like the only country in the world"; but straightway he finds a curious sickness, which he attributes to the exhaustion of the war. Sickness is on the ship coming out and, when he lands, the returning soldiers with him are curiously loth to rejoin their families and friends—"They won't mind waiting" says the soldier Johnson has been talking to. So the group of returned men spend the afternoon in the bar of the hotel, hugging to themselves the real human contacts which, they instinctively feel, are soon going to be taken from them. Yet this sickness is not just a result of the war. "There was a quietness and sickness over everything and over the other men in the bar." [8]

"Over everything." Mulgan, at the very beginning of his book, suggests that life in New Zealand is blighted and suffering from a deficiency of something. In the physical world there exists an equivalent for the moral deficiency disease which Mulgan intuitively diagnoses. In parts of the Upper Waikato Valley—the country around the lower slopes of Pirongia and Maungatautari, and the more intractable land towards the ranges east of Te Awamutu —there was, during the twenties and thirties, a soil condition known as "bush sickness." After the bush had been cleared and pasture sown, the land would yield quite fruitfully for a couple of years. But then the grass would stop growing. No matter how much fertilizer was used, growth would not begin again. Stock would grow weaker and finally die. Fern and scrub would creep

back into the pastures, and the desperate farmer would have to—
as the saying went—"walk off" his land. It was not until just before the Second World War that soil scientists diagnosed the disease as due to the lack of an infinitesimally small quantity of a
number of elements in the composition of the soil: the so-called
"trace elements," of which the most important was cobalt. The
addition of these substances to the dressings of superphosphate
which were normally applied to the pastures resulted in a miraculous and immediate resumption of grass growth. "Bush sickness" is
today a forgotten term in New Zealand, but something the same
as this Mulgan sensed as happening in the sphere of human relationships in New Zealand. Throughout the book we are constantly
reminded that in this country economics provides a grimly con-
stricting rule over human destinies.

CHAPTER 7

Portrait of a People

WITH unobtrusive precision *Man Alone* anatomizes the simple economic facts that dictate the pattern of New Zealand life. Looking for a job, Johnson surveys the "Situations Vacant" column in the daily newspaper; he discovers there are great numbers of situations vacant. As he reads, he hears a conversation between two farmers, the subject of which is the fantastic price of farm land. Here in a nutshell are the salient truths—a shortage of labor, the inflation of land values. These operate against ordinary human emotions because of the dominating urge which has laid hold on the inhabitants of the land—a lust to possess—to own a farm, a house, a sum of money in the bank.

Such an urge Mulgan shows at work almost universally—it is the economic *arrière-pensée* which crowds out humane feeling. It too has its origin in the pioneer's dream of possession: every man a landowner, every man a gentleman, every man a politician. The result, again in the words of Allen Curnow, has been ". . . Something different, something Nobody counted on." [1] Puritan and middle-class, the society Mulgan depicts in *Man Alone* is productive of a race that is strangely sub-human—possessed of the deficiency disease that robs them of grace, joy, and health, that makes their deepest emotions, their fondest dreams, relate to material advantage.

I A Farmer's Life

One of the praiseworthy things about *Man Alone* is the amount of space it gives to life in the country. When Mulgan's wife went to New Zealand in 1941 he warned her against judging the country on the evidence provided by the towns. "The real New Zealand," he wrote, "that so few people ever try to know is in the country. The trouble is that the country people are inarticulate

101

and only come to town to get drunk and go to the races so they do not make much impression on visitors." [2]

In his novel Johnson gains experience of a number of farms of different types. Constant in all is the stern economic imperative. Blakeway, Johnson's first employer, is the red-faced farmer he meets in the vestibule of the hotel. He gives Johnson a hard look and a searching cross-examination before reluctantly giving him a job. There is indeed a perfunctory nod towards motives other than economic. "I reckon we ought to help fellows that were in the war." [3] But the hotel clerk immediately afterwards gives the definitive verdict on Blakeway: ". . . He's mean as death." [4] On Blakeway's farm there is no mistaking the inhumanity of the pattern. The landscape strikes Johnson at once. The first three paragraphs of Chapter 2 sketch, with unerring conciseness, the tentative, half-formed quality of the countryside—"a green, rich, unfinished look . . . low hills, half-cleared . . . farm-houses wooden, unpainted." [5]

Masterly, too, is the description of the farm: the funereal pines, the featureless paddocks, the dark kitchen with the Victorian atmosphere: the monotony and blankness of an existence that "passed the first day as it did in all the three years he was there . . ." [6] And the telling sentence: "Milking at Blakeway's was as much like working in a factory as anything else." [7] In that sentence Mulgan has encapsulated the fate of the farmer who is a slave to production and nothing else. It is a twentieth century fate, and he shares it with girls in stocking factories and men in bicycle works. Johnson learns the nullity that accompanies it—summed up in the following paragraph:

He got to know the dates of the race meetings and where to get beer in town at most times, and the story of the 1905 match when Wales beat the All Blacks by one try to nil, and why it was necessary to have a farmers' government to protect the real interests of the country.[8]

The catalogue is familiar enough to all who know New Zealand. Fifteen years later M. K. Joseph was to repeat it in his "Secular Litany."

> Saint All Black
> Saint Monday raceday
> Saint Stabilisation
>   Pray for us.[9]

Johnson falls in with the aimless and insipid round of pleasure, the exhausting round of toil, which makes up life on the land. The remorseless rhythm of it all comes through Mulgan's prose: ". . . and all the time the warm rain came down and the grass grew thick and green and the cows came into the milking-shed heavy with cream." [10] What the system does to the individual is conveyed to Johnson in graphic terms while he is on Blakeway's farm, in the shape of Mabel's father and mother. "His face was grizzled over a drooping grey moustache, but the lines of his face were well formed and well fed. His wife, Mabel's mother, was a short plump woman with arms as powerful as a horse's leg but her feet were troubling her." [11] As Johnson looks at her, her husband speaks up: "There's only one thing you want to be a farmer . . . that's a good partner . . . like my old woman." [12] Johnson is immediately provoked into seeing himself and Mabel after two decades, in the unprepossessing couple before him. So that when Mabel echoes her father's opinions about the desirability of owning land, it is small wonder that "Johnson listened desultorily, having no ambition."

II *In Desperate Battle*

Yet the next farm Johnson goes to provides an even more striking cautionary figure, a living illustration of what the land can do to a man. This is Thompson, "a tall, gaunt riding-man." On his farm, in the steep hills between the Waikato and the west coast, the battle with the land is still being furiously waged. Here the imagery of war becomes explicit, for Thompson, a returned soldier, is locked in a desperate fury of combat. It is significant that in a way he confuses his present combat with the desperation of actual battle he has known. "He was going over it in his mind again, remembering every piece of it, the battles and the men and the names of places . . ." [13] The whole area is saturated with images of war and lonely death, and Scotty voices the opinion of a sane man when he says of Thompson, crazed and intense, working in blind fury inside his private dream of conflict: "He isn't human, Johnnie. He just isn't human." [14] Thompson, it is clear, is going to lose the battle with the land. Feverish energy is not enough: inexhaustible strength, inflexible will are not enough. The next farmer Johnson gets to know has these also. But he has something else besides.

This is Stenning, the King Country farmer whom Johnson meets when he has escaped from Auckland after the riots. He is just as single-minded as Thompson. Like Thompson, he has braced himself for total commitment in his struggle with the land, and Mulgan uses again the imagery of battle in association with the conflict. "What was real [to Stenning and Johnson] was the battle they were both fighting with the land they worked." [15] The difference between Stenning and Thompson is that the former has brought cunning to complement his doggedness. He has fathomed the economic rules that govern his existence, and is pitting himself against the predictable activity of banks and stock firms as well as the malicious passivity of the land. In Johnson he scents an ally, and takes him round the farm on horseback at an early opportunity . . . "trying to interest him in it." He succeeds. Not with words, for he is all but inarticulate; but with deeds, with the example of his sullen power. "[Johnson] admired his great forearms and his skill with an axe, and the way he drove at his work in a fury of accomplishment." [16] He never asks Johnson to follow him out to work, but Johnson never fails to do so. So that in the community of men with a common task Johnson experiences a relationship which is fuller of meaning than most of those he has encountered in New Zealand.

III   *Country Life*

This is not to say that Johnson's employer is shown as a particularly satisfactory human being. There is, in fact, a pathetic insufficiency in Stenning, the husband and head of the family. In his household the deficiency disease can be studied in its full flowering. Not only does Stenning not talk, but there is not the slightest of gestures towards civil behavior—neither physical comfort nor ease between fellow human beings. It is a heart-rending picture that Mulgan paints of a group of people thrust together in a private hell of incomprehension. All effort, emotional, physical, and economic, is offered up to the Moloch of the implacable land, so that Stenning, his wife, and his farmhand live in a social stone age. Mulgan's description, as usual, is brief but explicit:

Stenning never talked if he could help it, not even to Rua, and she would sit sulkily or play her few worn records on the gramophone until Johnson knew every scratch in them by heart. When Stenning swore at her, she would stop and give them a meal, banging and clattering with pots and burning the food, as likely as not, and then they would eat, silently and bad-temperedly. Johnson himself found Stenning trying on days like this. He would sit for hours before the fire, neither moving nor speaking, perhaps playing with his sheath-knife, sharpening it on the sole of his boot or carving wood shavings from a bit of firewood until the hearth in front of the range was littered with them. Then he would get up and perhaps look out of the windows at the fields and the rain, grunt heavily to himself, and sit down again.[17]

How gross is the barbarity of Stenning's household is demonstrated, with a dry pungency, by placing in contrast with it a few glimpses of the allegedly barbarous inhabitants of the country, Rua's Maori relatives from the village nearby. By Stenning they are despised: yet we sense in their behavior a quality of life that is lacking in Stenning's. In their haymaking, dancing, singing, and drinking there seems a primitive Arcadian quality that is ultimately life-enhancing. The rhythms of life impel them, not the grinding monotony of hard work for material gain. Yet even the latter, Mulgan suggests, has its moments of satisfaction, when, for brief periods, it coincides with the rhythm of life. In *Man Alone* one significant association is between life and the sun. When Johnson is in sunshine, there is usually a suggestion that he is following a vital pattern of existence.

Though in all probability unconscious on Mulgan's part, this imagery came from personal experience. Every year in Britain, he chafed at the virtual disappearance of the sun in the months of the English winter. By February he was usually in a state of profound depression. In late February, 1938 he wrote to his parents: "I don't think I can stay in this misty country for ever." However that may be, in the account of Johnson's work with Stenning, the sun appears to illumine the picture with brief happiness. "On good days, when the sun shone and the ground perhaps was hard and sharp with frost, it seemed the best life in the world."[18]

So Johnson experiences a kind of conditional satisfaction which arises out of the sense of achievement produced by common effort. Stenning has interested him by engaging his sympathy and challenging his manhood to accept the battle against the land. He is in a fair way to becoming a New Zealander, with all that that implies of harshness and inhumanity. Johnson responds with interest to Stenning's proposal that he should begin to rehabilitate the derelict farm across the river. But for the intervention of fate, in the shape of the killing of Stenning, Johnson would have settled in New Zealand.

IV   *The Urge to Acquire*

In doing so he would have yielded to pressures which began working on him as soon as he entered the country, and which were remorselessly applied to him wherever he went. He is expected to desire ownership; to act out the acquisitive bourgeois compulsions that disfigure the ordinary New Zealanders he meets, and which drain their responses of human warmth. How clearly this is stated may be seen from the opening sequence of the book. Johnson, a stranger, in the first chapter seeks the fundamental needs of food, sex, and work. In every case the response is sour and niggardly. The waitress who serves him "would not smile at him . . . resenting him and the work he caused her." The sad whore he meets is diseased; she goes off with another man. Blakeway grudgingly offers him his first job.

On the other hand, the facile companionship of the bar has its hard underside. When they hear of Johnson's having come from England, the group in the bar place him as a stock figure and try to interest him in buying land. Johnson is not interested. "I'm not looking to buy a farm. I'm looking for a job." [19] One of the men encourages him in his stand against ownership. Rough good nature is not far away, and Johnson is not permitted to pay for the drinks when he is found to be too short of money to put down a deposit on a farm. Such haphazard generosity only makes the fundamental selfishness of New Zealand society stand out in greater relief. Johnson sums up how little it really means, when he sees it first withering away in the hard frost of the depression.

Johnson felt the temper of the country changing. It had always been a lucky country, a country where, if a man were well and strong, he could wander about, and live well and eat well, where everybody was your friend in a hard, casual way, where a man tramping the roads in the back country could be sure of a night's rest and a meal wherever he stopped. It was strange to see how things changed now that the luck had turned, how people grew uneasy and careful with each other, and kept to themselves, watching and saving what they had.[20]

But before the depression the uneasiness and carefulness are apparent in some of Johnson's encounters. A grotesque incident involving a hotel-keeper and a retired Indian Army captain, comic in one way, retains a sinister undertone of cupidity. In the sun, amid the innocent pastoral setting of Northland, Johnson finds an idyllic peace not previously met with. "The tide was coming in over the mud-reaches pushing a line of foam with it and the mud-holes cracking open as it came. The air was soft and warm with a scent of pine and fern and warm mangrove mud. Only the moths and mosquitoes drawn to the lamp were a nuisance." [21] But his carefree gambling with the simple-minded old captain is a source of grief and dismay to the hotel-keeper, who threatens violence to Johnson after the latter has won a large sum from his guest. "You hand that over to me, you bastard. That's three weeks' board and lodging you got there . . ."

Johnson, unworried, moves on to his next job—even more idyllic than the peaceful hotel. This is aboard the "Sea Spray" where he works for a time as deckhand. "They were good days along the coast . . . They would sit there and smoke and talk, though not much, and watch the moon coming up in the sky and the lights ashore, and the riding-lights of the yachts and their own light on the mast-head shaking slowly across the sky." [22] Much of Johnson's satisfaction with his lot comes from the character of his captain, an old Swede called Petersen. Not much of a talker, "a simple man," Petersen has succeeded in establishing with Johnson a relationship that is vital, and rooted in life. The community of the sea has a good deal to do with this, the sense of comradeship independent of money. Yet even Petersen has been bitten by the bug of bourgeois acquisitiveness. He urges Johnson, "You got to start saving and looking after yourself some time." [23] Johnson, however, is still uncommitted. "He was in charge of himself and he did not worry." [24] He is, too, different from the pale young ex-soldier of Chapter 1: ". . . His skin bronzed and roughened and his hair bleached white. He was alive with the sun and the sleepiness of salt air and the long days at sea." [25]

V *A Civil Man*

For all his undemonstrative taciturnity, Johnson is a positive character. He brings with him, into his new environment, certain positive expectations of life. New Zealand fulfils these at first. The most important of them is freedom; the greatest threat to freedom is ownership. So Johnson resists ownership with great fortitude. He carefully preserves his right to work where he pleases and for whom he pleases, to move about and make friends where friendship is offering.

Furthermore, his positive demands on life go beyond the material. He is the only person in the book who responds with any kind of feeling to the appearance of the landscape. Twice in the book he looks with wonder at the snow peak of Ruapehu, and voices his excitement to a companion who looks at him uncomprehendingly. In the hills north of Raglan the far-off shadowy outline of the mountain is just visible. " 'It's a bloody marvellous country' he said. 'By God, Scotty, I wouldn't mind climbing that mountain there.' " [26] Scotty's reply is unsympathetic. "That's a daft idea," he says.

It can hardly be by chance that when working with Stenning, on the very flank of the great mountain which towers away from them, Johnson repeats his remark. "Did you ever climb that mountain?" he asks Stenning once, remembering how he had looked at it before with Scotty. "God no, now what would I be doing that for?" Stenning replies.[27]

It is clear that, in Mulgan's laconic notation, the mountain stands for very much more than itself—it is a symbol of the non-material values which Johnson stubbornly expects, coming as he does from an older society where some values transcend those of economic advantage. The same is true of the store he sets by the maritime life. He finds in it elements of experience which satisfy him, quite apart from the wages it provides.

Thus, although Johnson is an Everyman figure, he is not a simple one. His complexities are in a minor key, for Mulgan is determined on his averageness, and to make Johnson too much of an individual would mean enlarging his silhouette and lending it an heroic stance that would displace the interest from where it firmly remains—in the land and people we experience through Johnson.

CHAPTER 8

Individual and Society

BEHIND the figure of Johnson lies another interest of Mulgan's, perhaps a more profound one than the lineaments of his own country. From the time of the Auckland riots onward Mulgan was deeply concerned with the political ideology of Western Europe. The riots had been for him a revelation of the havoc which unjust and incompetent government could wreak on individual lives.

Preternaturally aware of the symptoms of social injustice, intellectually able to discern political incompetence through the smoke-screen of politicians' phrases, Mulgan found in England a social system more unjust than New Zealand's; but he found in it also a number of compensations of one kind or another. Obviously he was affected by such things as the brilliance of individual Oxford scholars, the civility of Oxford life, the great past of England evoked by buildings and place names. Yet he sought in English life a clue to the invincible vitality of England—the principle of life that had allowed England to dominate Europe for so long, in the face of all the palpable wrongs and miseries which its social system used to (and in many instances still did) embody. He could not think that this was a result of government by an élite, although this was the explanation complacently offered. From his own observations of the élite class, at Oxford and in London, he formed the opinion that it might well be in spite of, rather than because of, the élite that England had come through so well.

I   The Old Laborer

In one of the fragments of writing that survives from his Oxford days, Mulgan shows the kind of quality that seems to him to be necessary as a foundation of the good society. It is in a sketch entitled "Rustic Witness," composed, in all probability, as a newspaper article. This relates his chance meeting, in a country pub,

with a middle-aged farm laborer, whom he describes in these
terms:

He was a big man and broad-shouldered but past his youth. He had
come there fresh from his work, with worn coat and corduroy trousers
and the clay still clinging to his boots. His face was red with a deep
sunny glow, the skin roughened by wind and weather but curiously
fresh, and he had a moustache grizzled and drooping . . . He sat
there with one huge hand laid on the table beside a grey pewter mug
of ale and a massive square of bread, the other on his knee, and he
bent forward slightly as he sat, not in contemplation of anything but
strangely unregardful.

Mulgan talked to the man—about the weather, the district, and
his work. "Trees were his great affection. He had been grafting
fruit trees earlier in the day. Yes, he did a lot of grafting in the
district, had done for many years. He could make pippins grow
upon crab apples." The man had served (like Johnson) in the
Great War,

. . . in the county regiment . . . He had been in the beginning of
the Somme, and again at Passchendaele. There was nothing more to
say. He had been in the trenches, had probably killed men, had been
in long danger of life, and had suffered and endured but there was
nothing to say . . .
   And I knew then in what way his strength made him different from
other men I had known . . . He did not live in the oblivion of a peasant class, passing through life like the cattle of the fields. There was a
richness in his eyes and an intelligence in the quiet restraint of his
voice. He was aloof and apart in a curious and impregnable way. He
had not made the world into which he had been born, nor did he desire to alter it. He had accepted what men had imposed upon him, a
place in society and long labour; probably much suffering; never the
sharpness of actual poverty but always the hardship of pressing needs,
without remission. He had accepted all this and had been untouched
by it, and would go on, perhaps unconsciously a little scornful of the
world about him. He would be always dominant and undefeatable.[1]

In Part II of *Man Alone* these are the terms in which Johnson is
described—"wiry and reserved . . . grey but not beaten . . .
He had endurance." [2]
   The old farm laborer, in fact, became a kind of touchstone by

which to measure the efficacy of a system of government—that is, the measure of its success in permitting individual members of society to develop for themselves some richness and depth of life while remaining independent. "We searched," says Mulgan, in *Report on Experience,* "[in the prewar years] for something that could be both creative and stable." It seemed to him that in the way of life of the English farm laborer there was something of positive value. There is more than a suggestion that Johnson possesses, similarly, an inner fund of individual endurance and independence; and this gives him a melancholy dignity.

II *Widespread Avarice—and the Exceptions*

This quality is thrown into even more striking relief when Johnson emerges from his ordeal in the bush. With the exception of his friends the seafarers Petersen and Brown, every human soul Johnson meets is touched with the blight of cupidity: the mechanic who takes his sixpence in return for the use of the razor; the amazonian hoer of cabbages, who can give him a quarter of a row start and still beat him, and who rewards his afternoon's toil with a bundle of old clothes; the dispirited barman at Waiapapa. Finally, as he is taking a last glimpse of the country he is now leaving behind, the cockney steward tells him his own pathetic story—of the girl who has taken his presents and broken the engagement—which concentrates and enforces the theme which has been discursively developed all the way through the book. In the spiritual wilderness which Johnson finds New Zealand to be, the exceptions, who stand out in bold relief, are instructive. Like Johnson himself, they are men alone. There are only two of them. One is the sea captain, Petersen; the other is the old hermit, Bill Crawley.

Petersen lives by discipline and a puritan code. The counsel he gives Johnson to save his money and try to become his own master, to stop working for wages, is the common-sense result of experience. Yet the adoption of a bourgeois code of acquisitive capitalism has not corroded Petersen's humanity. The life of the sea has kept him sane and humane, if a little crusty and conventional. His defeat is, touchingly, a defeat by time. ". . . A new diesel engined and sail-less ship . . . covered their ground in half the time and always on time, with the roar of her engine shaking the cliffs . . ." [3] Petersen is of Victoria's reign, and in the closing

pages of Part I his straight-backed honesty and astringent com-
passion make both comic and touching the sequence in which a
berth is found for Johnson. This section of the book, when the
newspapers are carrying accounts of Johnson's being sighted
("There's nothing this country likes better than a good man-hunt,"
says Petersen) and when he is totally dependent on one man's
magnanimity, builds in suspense right up to the documentary account of the sail from one of the eastern bays on the north shore to
the Port of Auckland.

Just as Petersen embodies a precise and honorable code from
the past, so does the other solitary—Bill Crawley—look backward
to a now forgotten day—that of the pioneers. Like Petersen, too,
he provides a strong contrast to the prevailing materialistic tone
of New Zealand society. When Johnson staggers into his hut, his
response is typical. "Howdy mate . . . Come on in. Shut the
door." He recognizes Johnson's need, asks no questions, and min-
isters to him, giving up his bunk, clothing and feeding him. He is,
in fact, a practical Christian, though he would be likely to dis-
claim this. His is the archaic unwritten code of the early settlers,
when "Thou shalt help thy neighbour in his time of need" was the
law of life.

Furthermore, this code set much less store by human life than
the twentieth century does. In a mood slightly reminiscent of
Synge's *Playboy of the Western World,* the recital of Stenning's
murder elicits from Bill Crawley, not horror but amused admiration. "That's a bloody interesting story, son. I didn't know I was
entertaining such a bloody interesting fellow . . ." And Bill Crawley's advice to Johnson to consider bush-ranging as a profession—
"There's a good living there for an able-bodied man with a good
horse" [4]—while seriously offered, effectively shows us the wide
gap that separates the old hermit from twentieth-century life.

Both these men alone are independent and unbroken. There is a
third whom Johnson meets—an old tramp in a boxcar on a train.
He is, it is true, slightly daft. Yet in the context of the book he is a
menacing figure. Johnson first sees him surrounded with posses-
sions—"clothes, boots, two black tea billies, a shirt, a khaki scarf,
and a grey blanket." When he fails to offer Johnson any assistance,
the latter helps himself. The muttered remarks of the old hobo
complete the strangely menacing picture: for they are politico-
religious ejaculations ("Where is Christ now, and where is Cal-

vary" . . . "I knew Absalom, O Absalom, and Seddon, I knew Seddon"). The old tramp, in his crazy isolation, is a symbol of the society Johnson has found—protesting Christianity, talking brotherhood, but keeping his own to himself. He is the polar opposite of both Petersen and Crawley.

III *The Logic of Economics*

In these ways Mulgan exhibits and judges the social structure New Zealand has evolved. Materialism has distorted and pushed out of shape the pioneer settler's dream of an affluent egalitarian state. The hard facts are economic facts. Of these, the central one is that the whole material condition of New Zealand depends on an economic price being obtained for the primary products which come from New Zealand soil—for wool, meat, butter, cheese— when they are sold on world markets.

Johnson's early years in the Dominion display life when prices are high. But high prices mean, not ease, but anxiety. For then everyone wants a farm, and land prices rise. (The flood of soldiers returning from the war has intensified the process.) High land prices mean high interest rates on mortgages (as Stenning says, "Now who hasn't got a mortgage, in this country?"). So the farmer sees his returns being swallowed up, year by year. And a year or two of low prices will finish him.

Denis Glover's poem "The Magpies" incorporates the whole sad cycle.

> When Tom and Elizabeth took the farm
> The bracken made their bed.
> And Quardle oodle ardle wardle doodle
> The magpies said.
>
> Tom's hand was strong to the plough
> Elizabeth's lips were red.
> And Quardle oodle ardle wardle doodle
> The magpies said.
>
> Year in year out they worked
> While the pines grew overhead
> And Quardle oodle ardle wardle doodle
> The magpies said.

But all the beautiful crops soon went
To the mortgage man instead
And Quardle oodle ardle wardle doodle
The magpies said.

Elizabeth is dead now (it's years ago)
Old Tom went light in the head;
And Quardle oodle ardle wardle doodle
The magpies said.

The farm's still there. Mortgage corporations
Couldn't give it away.
And Quardle oodle ardle wardle doodle
The magpies say.[5]

The savagery of the land in its resistance to cultivation; the cupidity of men in their lust to possess; these two elements are allies in the warfare that goes on in the life of the average New Zealand farmer of the twenties and thirties.

IV   *The Character of the Land*

The physical outlines of New Zealand are unobtrusively present throughout *Man Alone*. It is as though Mulgan were providing a specific though unemphatic answer to *A Pilgrim's Way in New Zealand:* Johnson spends little time in the South Island, whose photogenic uninhabited tracts of mountain and forest have received their due in his father's work. But Johnson ranges widely in the North Island, where the less photogenic landscape—raw, savage, ugly—betrays the existence of the desperate war which is being waged. On his way to Stenning's farm Johnson feels himself in the heart of it. "Blackened trees still standing, blackened unrotted logs on the ground gave the hills the derelict air of a battlefield. Fire-swept, devastated country, broken and seamed, and showing clay where dry weather had caught it and cracked it." [6]

The battle against the land becomes actual during Johnson's flight and hiding after the murder. First the stone valleys of Ruapehu itself, then the howling pumice wilderness of the Rangipo Desert with "a sighing and moaning of wind and sand as it stirred in the corridors of the desert, more mournful and more frightening than anything human that he had known." [7] Then Johnson comes to the bush itself. "There was sound all the time, of the river running and birds from early morning to the owls calling at night, but he felt within himself a great solitude, a feeling which had never troubled him before in the long periods of his life that he had spent alone. There was a heaviness of the bush that pressed upon him and weighed him down, until the sound of his own voice was startling to him."

The account of Johnson's months in the bush has a documentary sobriety that makes it gripping to read. In its way, the account focuses with a peculiar clarity the desperation that the land engenders in its inhabitants. Johnson's feeling that he is unwilling to move, his acceptance of the "discomforts that had at first disturbed him," his attachment to the damp cave—"more comforting to him than most homes had been" [8]—these feelings are the same as the pioneers felt, only with Johnson they are raised to a higher power. The whole passage is a paradigm of the way of the land with the human intruder. Yet Johnson, as has been seen, carries with him in spite of all a strange affection for the country. The peace of Northland, the brooding presence of the great mountain on Stenning's farm, the radiant Hauraki Gulf with its green islands—these all gain Johnson's attention and to them he responds. The land is beautiful as well as harsh.

Objectively considered, Mulgan's account of the New Zealand that Johnson experiences is accurate enough. Gentle, sleepy, raw, ugly, beautiful, empty—the land wears all these faces. The comfortless bleak elements in the landscape are the ones that predominate: and we remember the original title—"Talking of War."

V *Imagery of Conflict*

The theme of battle emerges at various points—even in Johnson's first journey to the interior, where he is "seeing a new country open out like the raw edges of a wound." [9] It dominates the account of Thompson's farm, and the later account of Stenning's. After Johnson has killed Stenning ". . . it was like some old memory of the war that he had drowned." [10] His explanation of the death of Stenning to Petersen lays the blame on the conditions of life which the land imposed: "It came with working away on that farm, just the three of us, and no pay. None of us had any pay. You couldn't get away. You couldn't do anything but go on working. It wasn't any life." [11] To Petersen, too, Johnson puts in a nutshell the prevailing sense of being moved by forces that have unjustly exploited him. " 'I've worked hard all my life,' Johnson said, 'and been paid damn all.' " It is this grievance that lies behind the climactic violence of the riots, which precipitate Johnson's departure from Auckland.

Up till the time of the riots, Johnson has been shown as a docile, though not a submissive, character. He has sidestepped the strong inducement to marriage that Mabel holds out; he is not browbeaten by the hotel-keeper in Northland; he will not fall into the pattern of transient exploitation that passes for farming in New Zealand. "You didn't buy a farm and build a house and grow pinetrees round it to stay there, but to sell it to somebody else and live on the profit." [12] This is not for Johnson.

He is, in fact, a deceptively simple figure. Because of the reticent style, it is easy to mistake Johnson's stoicism for stupidity and insensibility. Neither of these attributes is his. He is unclouded by sentiment. And he has a kind of civility which inhibits him from throwing himself into the work and speculation fever which he finds gripping the New Zealanders, enslaving them and denying them freedom and maturity. He sees the land with the vision of an inhabitant of an older culture; he sees the potential of the land, in respect of a fully developed and splendid human life, and he sees that potential ignored in favor of a frenetic and ignoble helot's existence.

This attitude of Johnson's finds confirmation during the riots when the exaltation of concerted action gives way to shame as Johnson sees the looting begin. Then, heroically unselfish, Johnson risks his freedom and his life to rescue a friend. The narrative dealing with the riots is as condensed and telling as any in the book. Historians[13] have accepted its veracity as eyewitness detail. It is noteworthy that Mulgan has successfully transposed his point of view. In actuality he saw the riots as a special constable. In the narrative he has made an imaginative leap and put himself in the position of a rioter.

The riots sequence is one of the two peaks of violence that are reached in the course of the book. The other is Stenning's murder. Both of these peaks illustrate the violent effects of the distortions imposed on normal sensibilities by the false scale of values prevalent in New Zealand. Thus the riots show the results of mass starvation and deprivation. Society has lived by false materialistic gods. When they fall, it imposes savage restrictions on individual liberty. The result of these is a storm of collective anger in which men shake free from servitude. The release may be only temporary, but the magnitude of the deprivation was, one feels, unrealized even by Johnson as he joins the surge down Queen Street with the rioting mob.

Johnson went with them to the sound of glass breaking and women shrieking until he came to like it; past two men breaking a bottle of gin snatched from a hotel window over a lamp-post as they fought for it, and a woman stumbling back with her hand to her head; falling over a man who lay half on the pavement and half on the road, saying "Christ, Christ," to himself, and then swearing, too, because he had to say something; turning to see whether he could stop and know what was happening and then being driven forward again, knowing that it no longer mattered what happened while the whole street moved forward with him . . .[14]

What brings Johnson into trouble with the police, however, is not anonymous rioting but specific acts of hostility performed in the course of rescuing Scotty. Johnson's sense of values is delicately attuned: he feels ashamed of the looters. Their reversion to the endemic disease of cupidity almost, in his eyes, cancels out the grand disinterested statement of protest which the first rush had made.

VI *Marxist Slant?*

This section of the book has by some been seen (in conjunction with Johnson's journey, in Part II, to the Spanish War) as suggesting a Marxist moral; that Johnson's sense of power and purpose, derived from the march with his fellows up Queen Street, connotes an implicit endorsement of communism.

There is no real evidence for this. Johnson remains politically uncommitted. The nearest he comes to identifying himself with a Marxist outlook is one of the last things he says to Petersen just before he leaves New Zealand: "If fellows like me make more trouble now than they used to, it's because they've got more sense." Even after his arrival in England Johnson remains politically ingenuous. It is not until the Irishman O'Reilly interests him in the class struggle that he begins to see politics in Marxist terms. When he joins the International Brigade to go to the Spanish War, he reiterates: "I'm not a Communist, I'm a democrat." [15]

More significant than this perhaps is his acceptance of the label of New Zealander, which is attached to him by one of the party on the train. " 'E viva the government socialista of New Zealand,' said a little cockney opposite that Johnson knew." This acceptance gives perspective to Mulgan's picture of Johnson—"wiry and reserved, no longer eager but still living, grey but not beaten, moving impersonally and unquestioning through a world of which he had not yet understanding but which he could accept" [16]—we are reminded of the warfare that has toughened and annealed Johnson's manhood. The explicit conflict of the trenches in France is mentioned in the closing sequence of the book. One of his companions says to him: "Did you get this in the war—the Great War —marching off together?" " 'Maybe, I don't know,' Johnson said. 'It was a long time ago. I was young then. I was frightened a good deal of the time.' " [17] But his acceptance of the label "New Zealander" reminds us of the other warfare—the long, slow, furious engagement with the stubborn and beautiful land. This is what has helped to make Johnson what he is, a man capable of suffering and enduring.

CHAPTER 9

Man Alone—*Wider Implications*

ALL that Mulgan wrote of Johnson in extremity—"He didn't say anything . . . He didn't seem worried or unhappy. He was just sitting there . . ."[1] —came true four years later. In 1942, when Mulgan's battalion occupied positions in the Western Desert adjacent to the New Zealand Division, he had probably forgotten his description of Johnson. But what he wrote then about the New Zealanders as he saw them reminds us of that description.

Perhaps to have produced these men for this one time would be New Zealand's destiny. Everything that was good from that small, remote country had gone into them—sunshine and strength, good sense, patience, the versatility of practical men.[2]

"Everything that was good": we may note the implication that many things are not good. New Zealand is mentioned, in *Report on Experience,* with a gentleness of tone that strongly contrasts with the bitter undertones of *Man Alone.* By then the frustrations and injustices of Mulgan's youth had been long since exorcised by the writing of the novel.

Enough has been said to demonstrate the way in which contact with the humanist values of Western Europe brought into startling focus a vision of New Zealand which no writer had put down before Mulgan. It goes without saying that it is not the whole truth about the country. But there is sufficient disturbing relevance in Mulgan's vision to make it recognizable to a whole generation of New Zealand citizens who grew up between the wars. At a blow Mulgan destroyed the sanctified myth of the benevolent Motherland with her dutiful colonial offspring in the antipodes. He substituted a harsher, though truer, myth; for the world of *Man Alone* has the persuasive force and the coherence of myth.

This is so partly because of the formal excellence of *Man Alone:* as a novel it has subtlety and shape, which impart inevitability and narrative grace. Resting firmly on the solid foundation of the boldly original view of New Zealand society as discovered by Johnson, the narrative framework carries the interest, without strain or forcing, into the first climax—the raw intensity of the riots, with Johnson's pursuit and flight; then, in a swift surge of violence, into the sequence of Stenning's death and Johnson's second flight. In this latter part of the book the reader's interest is relentlessly engaged almost without intermission, until Johnson is on board the "Stamboulos," watching the New Zealand coastline recede.

It is the classic story-telling process—a first climax followed by a *détente;* a second climax; then a long and tense *dénouement.* Yet the beauty of *Man Alone's* performance is that the climaxes are functional—they arise from the data which is exhibited in the shape of the living conditions and the state of New Zealand society. Johnson is swept into the riots on the wave of a great mass movement of protest; he makes his individual statement, for a far from worthless reason (he irritates the police by attempting to help a comrade). Equally, he is forced into implication in the death of Stenning by reasons which are all too obvious (the peculiar rural craziness of a barbarous isolation). This peak of violence is prolonged into the long, cold violence of the land's attempt to destroy Johnson in the bush. Why does he survive? Mulgan nowhere states it explicitly, but we gain the impression that it is because he has inner resources which resemble those of the old English laborer whom Mulgan met in the thirties, and whose indomitable humanity won his respect.

Thus, Mulgan's achievement in *Man Alone* may in some respects be compared with those of the New Zealand poets of the thirties—of Curnow, Glover, and Fairburn, for instance. These men in their several ways sought to destroy the imperial myth and to discover the essential quality of the country they inhabited. None of them, however, have Mulgan's advantage of detachment; nor have they that calm disenchanted gaze which can measure the quality of New Zealand life against the richer and more varied patterns of life which Europe reveals.

In the wider view, *Man Alone* was a preliminary sketch by a painter whose subject was man in society. Determined to write only of what he personally knew, Mulgan was obsessed by the search for ways of solving the problem which he saw as fundamental for mankind: the problem of establishing a just society in which the individual could grow in reasonably civilized peace. As Dan Davin has put it: "The unemployed riots . . . for an honest ardent, generous mind . . . would never be over."

It was just about the time he graduated that Mulgan became aware that this search would have to be postponed. The lengthening shadow of fascism made it clear that the western democracies would sooner or later have to fight to preserve the conditions which, though far from ideal, did at least offer the possibility of amelioration for the common man. So it was that he made time to compose this passionate protest against the untrue picture of New Zealand which was current.

When he had to enlarge it, his preoccupation with the coming struggle against the dictatorships became dominant. But Part II should not be seen as a frame for Part I: merely as a tenuously relevant coda in which Mulgan has turned his eyes to the European horizon, and adumbrated the qualities of endurance which, in the succeeding seven years, were going to bring the democracies through. It is in these qualities that Johnson's unassuming hardihood is rooted: in the average man's essential will to resist oppression; that will which Churchill was to mobilize and direct when England stood alone in Europe against fascism. Thus, though it is a somber enough book in its way, the final statement is a hopeful one. Popular government has in it the potentiality of life; man can, in the ultimate analysis, control his fate.

CHAPTER 10

New Zealand—Report Revised

SEVEN years separate the writing of *Man Alone* from that of Mulgan's posthumously published book *Report on Experience*. The latter was begun after the author's return to Cairo from Greece in October, 1944, continued in Athens after his return thither in January, 1945, and concluded there two months later. The typescript he posted to his wife, with a covering letter, on March 19. In the letter he spoke deprecatingly of it as "only the draft and outline of a book I'd like to write." He suggested that the title might be "Summary of Experience."

When Gabrielle received the typescript, her husband was dead. She typed a fair copy of the original draft, and when she returned to England in September, 1945 she placed this in the hands of the Oxford University Press. After some delay, and a good deal of editing of Chapter 5 (on account of references to still living persons) the book was finally published, under the title *Report on Experience*[1] in the middle of 1947. It received favorable notices—notably a very sympathetic review in the *Observer* from Robert Henriques.

There are twelve chapters in the book. Three of them deal with the pre-war period, the rest with the experience of the war years. But the story of these years, though it deals in part with events such as those that inspired the writing of books like *Winged Dagger* or *Escape or Die*, is a thoughtful account of the events in which Mulgan participated, from a particular point of view. He reflected on what he had seen and done, in the light of the political and social problems which he had been ruminating on all his adult life. In the twelve chapters of this short book one has the impression of a man trying to set in order the immediate past he has lived through. It is as though Mulgan felt the need to assert that the horror and destruction he had witnessed was not in vain —that it had a purpose. He placed that purpose in the future, trying to link the future up again with the Marxist idealism of his youth in the past.

I *New Zealand Remembered*

The first chapter is interesting as defining the writer's attitude to his homeland. It contains the admission that, seven years before, he had rejected New Zealand and all it stood for, but that he now realizes that unconditional rejection is both fruitless and impossible. ". . . The land and the people whom we know when we are young stay with us and haunt us until we die . . ." [2] He reiterates in a general way the rootlessness of New Zealanders and their existence. "They live there like strangers or as men might in a dream that will one day wake and destroy them."

This sense of the land's brooding hostility Mulgan shares with his contemporary New Zealand poets Brasch and Curnow. Yet he remembers the landscape with a melancholy lyricism.

The country is, in fact, so old in itself that none of us have dared to touch it; we have only just begun to live there; the Maoris who came before us moved among the dark heavy trees like ghosts and could have sailed away at any time and never left a mark. We could leave it ourselves now. In a few years the red-roofed wooden bungalows would rot with borer and crumble into the earth. Fern would cover the grassland and, after fern, small trees would come and in time the dark, rich, matted bush again. Other men might come in a hundred years and nothing that we had left would worry them, but they could draw strength as we have done from the sharp fierce lines of the hills and the streams always running and the wide sea on every side. [3]

Paradoxically, the sense of security which New Zealand generates becomes oppressive, in Mulgan's opinion. The sense of a life outside is conveyed in the image of the Pacific Ocean, which surrounds the islands:

a long, deep and monotonous swell rides in at the end of a long journey. New Zealanders are all the time standing on the edge of these seas. They spend their lives wanting to set out across the wide oceans that surround them in order to find the rest of the world. [4]

Substantially, Mulgan's account of New Zealand repeats the picture already drawn in *Man Alone*—but without the pitilessly scathing tone. Here Mulgan is tolerant—even gentle.

New Zealanders don't like having their deficiencies pointed out to them—who does? They never tried to glory in their lack of culture, but I don't think they minded not having any.[5]

He sees the heedless happiness of life between the wars removed at a blow by the depression, which for the first time brought trouble "on a large scale" to the Dominion. This trouble he relates to the wider political forces then beginning to move: the rise of fascism in Italy and Germany, the New Deal in the U.S., the outbreak of the Abyssinian War.

What stands out for him in these events is their remoteness from New Zealand—or, rather, the remoteness and insignificance of New Zealand, locked in its dream of security and well-being. His account reads scornfully of life there after the depression has been "by successive stratagems" circumvented: "I am told on good authority that beer and horse-racing remained in favour in New Zealand. There were hot summers and some very debatable football." [6]

He is honest enough to relate how events caused him to revise this jocular opinion. "Afterwards, a long time afterwards, I met the New Zealanders again, in the desert below Ruweisat Ridge, the summer of 1942." [7] There follows an account of how the New Zealand Division, at the critical balancing moment of the see-saw which was the North African campaign, was the decisive element in keeping Rommel out of the Nile Delta, and so ultimately in winning the war.

The novelty of seeing his homeland as a significant force in world affairs shocked Mulgan into a closer look at the soldiers who had brought about such a result, and the organization that had made it possible. From his contemptuous dismissal of New Zealand as comically unimportant, to the realization that, in the critical moment of the drama he had so long awaited, they had delivered the decisive act, was a jump almost as great as Yeats's sense of the "casual comedy" of Irish life being turned into "a terrible beauty."

It seemed to me, meeting them again, friends grown a little older, more self-assured, hearing again those soft, inflected voices, the repetitions of slow, drawling slang, that perhaps to have produced these men for this one time would be New Zealand's destiny. Everything that was good from that small remote country had gone into them—sunshine and strength, good sense, patience, the versatility of practical men. And they marched into history.[8]

And yet, the fundamental unimportance of the country remains for Mulgan. Great events will be played out, the destiny of the world be decided, far away from the South Seas. Subtly and gently at the end of Chapter 1 he returns New Zealand to the limbo where he thinks it belongs. In a rather perfunctory paragraph he assigns it the role of fairy-tale elysium:

If the old world ends now with this war, as well it may, I have had visions and dreamed dreams of another New Zealand that might grow into the future on the foundations of the old. This country would have more people to share it. They would be hard-working peasants from Europe that know good land, craftsmen that love making things with their own hands, and all men who want the freedom that comes from an ordered, just community. There would be more children in the sands and sunshine, more small farms, gardens and cottages. Girls would wear bright dresses, men would talk quietly together. Few would be rich, none would be poor. They would fill the land and make it a nation.[9]

It is hard to be other than skeptical about this piece of sentiment. Mulgan's patronizing attitude towards New Zealand is made more clear if we look at the passage immediately following Chapter 1. In this he bitterly reproaches his father's generation for foisting a sentimentalized picture of England on to his generation. Yet he has just applied the same technique to his visionary New Zealand of the future. The irony is unconscious, but the intention is clear—he has paid some tribute to the land of his birth and can henceforth forget it.

II *A Portrait of England*

What he turns to in Chapter 2 is England; the gulf between the childhood legend and the reality he experienced as a young man, the inevitable vision of war, and the quality of the events that led towards it. The journalistic overtones of some of Mulgan's newsletters and special articles may be heard in this chapter. Yet the material is fundamental enough. Instead of the land of gentleness and mellow beauty that his boyhood stories had glorified, he found a land "of facile, emotionless suburbs"; ". . . a caste system more rigid than the Hindu"; political power in the hands of the middle class, who "played for safety at every turn."

Mulgan sees the central defect in English life as the abdication, by the people of England, of their responsibility, so that "the men who got things done, the wise fellows, the professionals, the self-selected . . ." were left in control. He thinks that personal inclinations, running uncontrolled, began the disastrous process.

It was clear enough what each would do, how one would rearm the enemy for profits in cash, another hold back from opposing him for fear of endangering the sacred traditions of property, yet a third refuse to provide defences for fear of the two edged weapons that his native opponents might obtain, a fourth grow pacifist from abhorrence of the facts of war.[10]

Thus Mulgan attributes to the people of England a kind of relief, when war came, "an element of expiation, the pride of a people that had watched in silence, strangled and hushed by their leaders, the endurance of Madrid and Barcelona, Shanghai and Chungking, and could now share as veterans in their own right the same communion of suffering." [11]

In a brilliantly crazy collage of facts and impressions Mulgan gives a highly colored account of the drift towards war in the thirties. But in the following chapter he opposes, to the phantasmagoric diversity of these events, the unity of the searching mind. He is speaking for the thousands of intelligent men all over Europe who saw the approach of disaster and sought a way out of it. Soberly he narrates his own experience in New Zealand of what he suspects to have been a worldwide pattern.

The Great War—the first Great War—cut deep into a generation of men and tired out those who survived. In the bad years there was a wide gulf between the ignorance of our youth and the old men who had run the country for so long . . . Between the two generations there grew up a genuine hatred, rare and peculiar to those times.

And he goes on to revolve, meditatively, the kinds of faith which the young were offered in those days—the Oxford Group, Fascism, Communism. Of these, he says "Only Marx in our time had church, gospel and following." [12]

CHAPTER 11

Social Structures in War and Peace

MULGAN makes it clear that, though he may have been one of the Marxist congregation ("There wasn't anywhere else to go," he says—"except to the pictures—and the publichouses; where, to be frank, I also spent a good deal of my time.") he nevertheless had taken note of the inconsistency of communist politics, and the inhumanity of the general communist outlook. "Their treatment of individuals was too coldly impersonal to offer much hope of a free and fair world." He thought English communists "soft—by continental standards." He wonders, in his calm way, at the intellectuals "who went into the party like novices dedicated to a church." He found himself "again doubtful of a political system that embraces men so willing to escape from themselves, that offers this easy answer and refuge from decision." [1]

When Mulgan speaks, in this chapter, of "the search that we made for a political religion and belief" one cannot doubt his sincerity. In Davin's words, for Mulgan the Auckland riots would never be over. But over the search fell the shadow of the war, and the last section of Chapter 3 gives a sense of the way in which forces larger than individual men hurl individual lives into confusion. ". . . History, turning us over with the momentum of an ocean wave, threw us belatedly with Russians, Chinese, Americans, the disarmed millions of Europe, into a combined fight for survival . . ." [2] The bitterest thought, to Mulgan, is the utter ineffectualness of everything done in Britain in the thirties.

We found nothing for ourselves. In the end the war came to meet us and we fought it for our own defence. Nothing of the heart-ache and struggle for belief in the decade before the war bore any fruit. Only as we began to win the war did we realize this and know that we would have to begin to think positively again. [3]

I *The Military Microcosm*

What Mulgan has observed from his six years in the British Army (a longer time, after all, than he spent in his Oxford college) is embodied in the following two chapters. Independent and observant as ever, Mulgan refused to be blinkered by his commissioned rank. He looked objectively at the time-hallowed army procedures which he was called on to operate, he evaluated from the private soldier's point of view the effectiveness of the training system, he ranged his level gaze on his brother officers and pondered their efficiency in doing their job.

For, as he saw, "once war starts, the British Army becomes the British nation." [4] The social structure of military life is a microcosm of the national social structure. Mulgan was scathing about both.

After the Great War, the British appear to have decided that their army was inefficient, but that this was something like an act of God or a decision of nature that couldn't be altered . . . They left themselves with little cause for complaint when the Second Great War started, since a country on the whole gets the Army it deserves, and the British certainly deserved this one. [5]

The one element of value which Mulgan found in the Army was "a system . . . of feeding and caring for a number of men and knowing how to carry out the detail of orders. The exponents of this system were the regular soldiers and N.C.O.'s and they must have derived it in unbroken tradition from a long way back." [6] To these men he pays a touching tribute.

Behind them lay the eternal gossip of military communities, the struggle to have children and home, a future of small pensions and menial jobs in civil life. But the bitterness and the system produced an austerity which is useful for war, and you thanked God when you met them—the straightbacked, humourless, reliable men, without imagination, but also without temperament, who do what they say they will do and often get killed in the process. [7]

He found something to admire, too, in the independence and assurance of the technicians who were now to be found in the army. But the chief defect of the British Army he found to be the incompetence and incomprehension of its officer class.

The young gentlemen of England do their best, of course. They always do their best, particularly in war-time . . . But their ignorance is wide and alarming, and their acceptance of a social framework is as instinctive as the act of breathing.[8]

It was, in fact, in the social framework that he found the chief defect.

. . . It is clear that the one good reason for the existence of a better-favoured class is that it should do the work that it has been chosen and educated to do. There is a lot to be said for having a small number of people about with nice accents and a sense of authority, but they need to realize why they are there.[9]

Nevertheless, the development of better understanding between officers and other ranks which had taken place in the Eighth Army Mulgan saw as a hopeful sign.

There still remains for me a vision of that sun-tried Desert Army, as a model of what men in the ugly business of fighting should attain to; and behind this belief lies a hope that this might remain as a lesson and an ideal.[10]

The lesson and the ideal are social as well as military. Mulgan sees the imperative necessity of bringing status and merit more closely into line in English society than they have formerly been.

Documentation of extreme examples of this defect is to be found in Chapter 5, which deals with the three battalion commanders under whom Mulgan served in the Middle East. The original draft contained more rigorous criticism than appears in the printed text of *Report on Experience*. The first colonel was a regular officer whose firm belief was that fighting was only hindered by planning and staff work. Mulgan says:

I remember one evening on board [on the voyage out] when he had been unfavourably compared with some of his colleagues over some question of military theory, his calling me into his cabin on my way to bed, inviting me to drink to the confusion of all military theorists.

"I can't argue with them," he said. "They can keep all their Staff College paper. But I'll be interested to see them there when the shells start falling."

He was, I remember, very excited over this. "By God yes," he said. "When the mortars come down whee-e-e" and he made a sweeping gesture with his hand that cracked the glass on the cabin basin. "You'll see only fighting if you come with me," he said, "just ordinary fighting, by God, no three-page orders." So we shook hands on that, two tough fellows that were just going to go and fight, and not worry about any military theory.[11]

The first occasion on which the battalion went into action, however, was disastrous. The lack of a workable plan meant that their night attack brought heavy casualties, and left the remnant of the unit in a vulnerable position all the next day. As a result,

The whole battalion had to be made over again. A few days later the colonel who commanded us left. I don't know why, or who decided he should go, or even where he went. I never saw him again . . . I expect he had better and luckier times later in the war . . .[12]

Fortunately, his replacement was a thorough soldier. "He took us into the battle of Alamein and made it by comparison a picnic." Slowly, the battalion regained confidence.

But whoever knew them or remembered their recent history would have known that this new confidence was delicately balanced against an old despair. They would have known, too, that as a battalion they were suspicious of colonels.[13]

The fact that, when this second colonel left, the replacement commander had never led a fighting battalion was not so bad. What appalled Mulgan was the utter lack of thinking power which he demonstrated. Mulgan is pleased, for the sake of the battalion, that his unilateral action in complaining to higher authority and resigning from the battalion led to a better man being appointed, and to the continuance of the battalion as an efficient fighting unit. He sums up the question of leadership by saying, "men would forgive any vices in a commander so long as he was capable." [14]

II   Conviction and Courage

The next chapter deals with some of Mulgan's thoughts about the relationship between belief and the will to fight. He comments on the solidarity of the English as a nation—"The English are a family and at every crisis of their family life, like a wedding or a funeral or an eviction, they act as one." He distinguishes between the armies of the past that have fought well from desperation and those that have fought well from a sense of their own superiority.

But the universal quality Mulgan thinks he detects in successful armies is something he calls "the organization of courage." It comes, he says "from being part of a body of men who rely on each other and move together." It is an essential ingredient, he maintains, in the effective functioning of small fighting units, though on a wider scale it could be felt only occasionally and never for long. He mentions two or three examples of sensing "that we were part of a movement that was as wide as the earth, and a part of all humanity." [15] One is the spectacle of the first assembly of the convoy in which he sailed to the Middle East— "whichever way you looked there seemed to be ships breaking the seas together, and you could feel then, not for the first or the last time, this warmth in being part of a great enterprise." [16] Another occasion was his journey by R.A.F. plane to parachute into the mountains of Greece—"feeling yourself again part of an organization that was cool and efficient and would in the end break open the fortress of Europe . . ." [17] Later, too, when the R.A.F. brought air-drops of supplies—tenuously and uncertainly for a start, but later with greater regularity—he sensed the power that a felt common purpose could impart to the individual.

It is clear that Mulgan sees this military virtue as possessing civil and social relevance. It is necessary, as he points out in the final chapter of the book, for men to feel some purpose in their lives, to sense that their work is productively organized. The development of effective morale among fighting troops has, he thinks, direct relevance to the development of effective morale among the working members of a nation. This is what worries him as he surveys the manner in which, after 1943, the military organization of men and materials has progressed. He feels that the war is going to be won all right but that, after all, the political vacuum that existed in 1939 is still going to be there. But he digresses for a chapter to contrast the English nation, once committed to the war, going into it with decision and solidarity, with the Italian, which played at being a military nation, without any mature understanding of the harsh ultimate reality that this involved.

III *Tragic Dilemma in Greece*

The two chapters which follow treat of underground warfare as Mulgan experienced it in German-held Greece. His account is marked by its relaxed and reflective understatement. His own exploits are hardly mentioned. What is in the foreground, in his account, is the Greek population. Thus in Chapter 8 he gives an account of the economy of a Greek mountain village, pointing out the precarious way in which, even in good times, the population is able to live.

But a plague of locusts or a snow-storm in May, or a war, means disruption, and then people start to die, first the very old and the very young and the sick, and after that the ordinary strong peasant men and women also die.[18]

What comes through in these chapters is the bitterness of Mulgan's dilemma in having to decide on individual acts of sabotage which, he knew, would bring terror and destruction on the heads of the civil population. From these acts he could not, of course, turn back. It was what he was there for. But the writing betrays some of the disquiet Mulgan felt—guilt that he should be responsible for bringing misfortune on the Greeks, mixed with profound admiration for their endurance and their uncompromising resistance. Eventually they completely captured his heart and imagination. In his terse laconic style he gives three examples, in Chapter 9, of the kind of individual he met, and he sums up in these words: "There was some quality in these people as there is, I expect, in all simple peasant people, that was solid and indestructible." And he tells the story of Kaitsa, where the people ask him, not to call off his demolitions, but make them on a scale great enough to justify the destructive retribution which they know will inevitably follow.

As a result, of course, Mulgan mounted his most ambitious attack on the Germans, which failed through a leakage of information. But this and other incidents—in fact, the whole narrative of his life in occupied Greece—is related in the barest outline. The climax is the last rampage of the S.S. up the Sperkheios Valley when over forty villages were deliberately and ruthlessly destroyed. Mulgan's deep disquiet resounds in the melancholy of the concluding paragraph telling of his ride to Lamia after the Germans had left. "The road we travelled was lined with graves we could not see, and for each person that shook us by the hand we could imagine a son or a brother who should have been there to shelter us from reproach, and was not there—being dead." [19]

A different kind of disquiet penetrates Chapter 10, on the nature of communism as observed in the Greek mountains. The campaign of propaganda and terror by which ELAS kept control of the mountain villages was something the B.L.O.'s were powerless to interfere with. Mulgan admits, "We bought them into complaisance and left them free to run politics in the mountains so long as we were permitted—and it required permission—to fight the Germans on the railway line." [20] He sees the ultimate element in the undemocratic exercise of power as "the terror which overshadows men's lives . . . Mostly, it comes down to cases with two strongarm men who call round and offer a beating-up or a contribution to the party chest." [21]

It was the aftermath of the struggle against this power that Mulgan found when he returned in January, 1945. He describes in Chapter 11 the sad face of Athens at that time, and his frustration at seeing fine men who had worked tirelessly for his organization against the Germans shot down by the communists. In this chapter, too, comes the epic story of Fafoutis, the Greek fisherman of Euboea who began by casually hiding Allied servicemen and ended by becoming, against his will, an Allied agent. The Germans had caught and beaten him. His village was a hundred and fifty miles from Athens and he ends up his narrative: "I don't remember well any longer; after the Germans caught me and beat me, my eye hurts me and I do not remember. But I remember that I went thirteen times the road from my village to Athens and brought out many men." [22] The last journey that Mulgan made, in Greece, was to visit the mother of Fafoutis, in a village near Kymi, where she lived.

IV *Government for Humans*

Mulgan's conclusion, in the twelfth and last chapter, concerns the question he has raised in Chapter 7—"the way men should live and how they should behave to one another." He begins with something that is certain—the opinions he has heard sincerely voiced by the ordinary men he has commanded. These opinions embodied wishes that were far from extravagant. "Every sensible man wants a home and the woman that he wants to live with and room for his children to move in. And besides that he wants some work to do." [23]

Mulgan suggests that these requirements might be made the starting point of the political organization of the postwar era, for he sees the great deprivation of the war as the snatching of ordinary family life away from practically the whole British nation. He sees this family life as the foundation on which any political system should be based. "If we can have the freedom to love someone that is sufficient to begin with." [24] He believes strongly, too, that the English political system has in it the possibility of good sense: that the demands of the ordinary man are likely to be more unyielding, the understanding of the governing classes more tolerant, than before the war.

CHAPTER 12

Conclusions

CAUTIOUS and diffident, Mulgan's assay of possible future political development is, one feels, indebted to two particular impressions. One was the example of the New Zealand Division, which he saw as a paradigm of the just—and efficient—society; a society in which the right to govern bore some relation to the ability to govern, and where the obligation of serving was freely accepted by free men. The other impression was the sense of intense life which he gained from his contact with the Greeks—a life which irradiated with vital flame the elemental facts of living. This intensity (personified and immortalized by Kazantzakis in the figure of Zorba) was felt poignantly by Mulgan, in Athens in March, 1945, as he came to the end of his brief draft.

The sparse green of Attica and the rare fruit blossoms in the city of Athens never looked or smelled sweeter in all their long history than they did in the last spring of the great European War when we began to make plans for a new Europe and a new world.[1]

In his letter which accompanied the draft of *Report on Experience* Mulgan called it "the draft and outline of a book I'd like to write." The model he had in mind was C. E. Montague's *Disenchantment*.[2] Montague had been outraged by the suffering of the fighting men in World War I, and sickened by the selfishness, hypocrisy, and muddle which caused it. For the latter he indicted the whole system of British society. He talks of "sitting after sitting of the dismal court that liquidated in the Flanders mud our ruling classes' wasted decades . . ."[3] And he makes a strong plea for a sense of the goodness of the ordinary things of life: "we each have to fall back, with a will, on the only way of life in which the sane simplicity of joy in plain things and in common rightness of action can be generated."[4]

Like *Disenchantment, Report on Experience* is in reality a series of essays. In the former book the framework into which these are fitted is a vaguely chronological account of World War I; in the latter, it is a vaguely autobiographical narrative. In the nature of things, therefore, Mulgan's range tends to be wider. In fact, he has written the "draft and outline," not of one book, but of three.

The first is clearly a book about New Zealand. He would unquestionably have written perceptively had he revisited that country, and have added something to the statement contained in *Man Alone*. But the center of his thought is England, not New Zealand. He had a keen interest in the way in which postwar English society was likely to develop, an interest which showed that his remaining with the British Army was an act of choice. He would have written with wisdom on English politics. Finally, he would also obviously have been capable of writing on Greece and her people, for his affection is eloquent in almost all the references he makes to that country.

So we are left asking, as at the end of Part I, why did this man, wise and patient beyond his years, courageous and steadfast in every job he had ever had to do, take his own life just ten days before the peace that would have released him once more to creative, humane activities? The question, of course, is unanswerable. The nearest guess one may hazard is that the strain of the struggle had been too great for a lively, alert imagination. In the course of its last convulsion, World War II claimed one of the last, and one of the least able to be spared, of its many victims.

Small and fragmentary though Mulgan's output may be, it is sufficient to assure him of consideration when the beginnings of New Zealand literature are discussed. For he was the first to formulate and to bring into literary focus the theme of the interlocking complexities of individual, human society, and landscape in New Zealand. Writers as varied as James K. Baxter, Maurice Duggan, Maurice Shadbolt, and C. K. Stead have touched upon it since, and have shown that the theme is central in the consciousness of New Zealand.

Notes and References

Chapter Two

1. *The Wellingtonian*, LXII, pp. 11–12.
2. Arthur Nicholson to Alan Mulgan, July 27, 1929.
3. From an unpublished typescript.
4. E. H. Blow to the author.
5. Professor R. P. Anschutz to the author.
6. Associate-Professor J. M. Bertram to the author.
7. *Craccum*, May 10, 1932, pp. 1–2.
8. D. M. Davin, review of *Report on Experience, Landfall* (March, 1948), 50–55.
9. Associate-Professor J. M. Bertram to the author.
10. Alan Mulgan's account of the Rhodes Scholarship was compiled four months after his son's death. The text of it is as follows (a passage describing the careers of Cox and Bertram has been omitted):

The facts about John Mulgan's experience of nomination for the Rhodes Scholarship should be put on record, for two reasons. It is not only that an exceptionally good candidate was passed over twice, but that his treatment throws light on the possibilities of professorial behaviour. If his case were merely one of opinion for and against a candidate, it would not merit setting forth. There must have been numbers of Rhodes candidates whose families and friends considered they should not have been passed over, but the decision was taken in a sporting spirit and quickly forgotten. John Mulgan's case was different.

When he was a second-year student at Auckland University College, he was chosen as one of the College's two nominees in 1931. It is customary in New Zealand for the Colleges to nominate, and the Selection Board to choose, graduates. John Mulgan's nomination was therefore unusual, and a clear indication of his standing in the eyes of the authorities. The other Auckland nominee was James Bertram. When the Selection Board in Wellington made its choice of Bertram and Geoffrey Cox (from Otago) John Mulgan was called before the Board. He was told that some of the members had wanted to choose him, but the fact that he was young and would have another opportunity weighed in the decision. The Board hoped he would come before them again. One of the members said afterwards that they had been "thrilled" to get such a candidate. John's family had no quarrel with the decision. Bertram and Cox were both older men with excellent records. They justified their selection. . . .

In the following year, 1932, the Professorial Board of Auckland University College had again to nominate two students for Rhodes Scholarships. Mulgan was again a candidate, and it was generally taken for granted that he would be nominated, but the voting placed him third. Preferential voting was used for the first time in such selections, and it seems certain that some members of the Board did not use the system intelligently. They assumed that Mulgan would be placed first, and concentrated on the other candidates. When the meeting broke up several of the members went to Mulgan, expressed their regret at what had happened, and wondered if anything could be done about it. Nothing could be done. The meeting was held early in the afternoon, and the names of the nominees appeared shortly after in the local evening paper.

One professor is reported to have said that day that this was the worst thing that had happened since he came to the College. Another rang me that evening, and described John's rejection as "a gross miscarriage of justice." Attempts were made, largely by this second professor, to get another nomination. There was a lot of feeling in the College, but of course the subject could not be ventilated in public. I had introduced John to "Mr Dooley's" superb burlesque of the Dreyfus case, and one day during the excitement, he applied a passage in it to himself. "If I was prisident iv this coort-martial, I'd say to Cap Dhryfuss; 'Cap, get out. Ye may not be a thraitor, but ye're worse. Ye're become a bore.'" There was a stir in the public, however, when it was announced that the Selection Board decided to make no choice of Rhodes Scholars that year, because no candidate was good enough. This had never happened before.

John Mulgan had a third chance in 1933. In the interval there was a very warm election to the College Council on the issue of freedom of speech. A member of the Council who favoured restriction on such freedom stood for re-election, and was opposed by a leading lawyer, who made freedom his platform. Feeling ran high inside and outside the College. This was during the economic depression, when there was much fear of what was called Bolshevism, and Left thinking generally, and their effects on the wage-earning class, especially the large number who were not earning. There were manifestoes and counter-manifestoes. Through a misunderstanding, the president of the Students' Association signed an anti-freedom circular, and John Mulgan and other members of the executive of the Association considered it their duty to sign one on the other side, so that the public would not be led to believe that the Association stood for restriction. I remember well the evening John came home and told us what he had done. Knowing how bitter the feeling was, I said to myself (but only to myself and afterwards to my wife): "My lad, this will cost you the Rhodes nomination." I was right. John was not nominated in 1933. Immediately the nominations were made, he went to Oxford and entered at Merton. One of the first things he noticed at Oxford was a poster announcing a meeting in favour of freedom of speech.

It is likely that the action of the Selection Board in not choosing anyone the previous year, annoyed some members of the Auckland Professorial Board. They may have taken this as an ultimatum that if the Board could not get John Mulgan, they would not take anyone. I am convinced, however, that the freedom of speech controversy was the main factor. The two professors I have mentioned were both in the anti-freedom camp. Despite the sympathy they showed for John after the non-nomination in 1932, before the controversy arose, they never displayed to me the slightest interest in him after that battle. I was known to both of them, and indeed I was a colleague of theirs—though a very minor one—on the College staff. They never expressed any regret about his second non-nomination, enquired how he was getting on at Oxford or in his subsequent career, or congratulated me on his successes. Indeed from the time of the fight over freedom of speech to this day, neither has mentioned his name to me. John seems to have been regarded in certain quarters as "a dangerous fellow." Really he was not a Communist at all, but a Liberal.

Some years later I was talking to the late Harold Mahon, who had been John's headmaster at the Auckland Grammar School, and on his retirement became President of the Auckland College Council. Mahon had the highest opinion of John, and was deeply interested in his career. He regarded John as the best all-round boy he had had through his hands. He went to see John at Merton, and was impressed by his standing there. This, I think, was the last time I saw a man I greatly admired and liked, for not long afterwards he died suddenly. We talked of John and I said I thought he lost the nomination through his part in the controversy. Mahon replied with emphasis: "I know he did."

This is the story of what Geoffrey Cox, himself a Rhodes Scholar, and a friend of John's, writing after John's death, described as a "ridiculous and cruel muddle." John developed on the other side of the world the powers he showed here. He was scholar, publicist, man of affairs, soldier, and born leader of men—just the combination Cecil Rhodes had in mind. The injustice was done by a body of men who may be supposed to have more than average intelligence and sense of responsibility.

11. *Auckland Star,* May 25, 1933.

12. See Alan Mulgan's account, Note 10 above.

13. To his parents, n.d., postmarked November 22, 1933.

14. Now Sir Geoffrey Cox, Director of News Services, I.T.V.

15. Now Associate-Professor J. M. Bertram, Victoria University of Wellington, New Zealand.

16. To his parents, November 22, 1933.

17. Letter to the author, March 3, 1964.

18. *Auckland Star,* December 1, 1934; December 8, 1934; December 15, 1934.

19. To his parents, February 13, 1934.

20. To his parents, May 29, 1934.

21. *Ibid.*

22. To his parents, July 3, 1934.

23. On October 6, 1934; October 13, 1934; October 20, 1934; October 27, 1934; November 3, 1934.

24. To his father, October 9, 1934.

25. Now Merton Professor of English Language, Oxford University.

26. Mr. Colin Reeve in a letter to the author, January 2, 1964.

27. "London Christmas," *Auckland Star,* February 9, 1935.

28. To his sister, January 4, 1935.

29. To his parents, May 26, 1935.

30. Dr. K. Sisam to the author, March 23, 1964.

31. Now President of Trinity College, Oxford.

32. A. L. P. Norrington to the author, December 27, 1963.

33. Dr. K. Sisam to the author, March 23, 1964.

34. To his father, December 15, 1935.

35. To his parents, January 29, 1936.

36. A. L. P. Norrington to the author, December 27, 1963.

37. To his parents, August 20, 1937.

38. To his parents, February 26, 1938.

39. E. T. Williams, now Warden of Rhodes House, Oxford.

40. To his father, April 3, 1938.

41. To his parents, September 7, 1938.

42. Now Vice-Chancellor, University of Auckland, New Zealand.

43. To his parents, September 19, 1939.

Chapter Three

1. To his wife, May 11, 1941.

2. To his wife, August 22, 1941.

3. London, 1946.

4. *Apple of Discord* (London, 1948), pp. 72–73.

5. *Report on Experience* (London, 1948), p. 89 (hereinafter abbreviated as *R.E.*).

6. *Apple of Discord,* p. 167.

7. *R.E.,* p. 93.

8. *Ibid.,* p. 95.

9. *Ibid.,* p. 97.

10. Major Michael Ward to the author, February 3, 1965.

11. British Liaison Officer, the official title of British officers dropped into Greece.

12. *Greek Entanglement* (London, 1955).

13. Professor N. G. Hammond to the author, 1964.

14. *R.E.,* p. 104.

15. Mr. Alfred Borgmann of Nashville, Tennessee, to the author, 1964.

16. *R.E.,* pp. 114–15.

17. In a letter to the author, 1964.

18. *R.E.,* p. 112.

19. *Ibid.,* p. 113.

20. *Ibid.*

21. *Ibid.,* p. 116.

22. To his wife, November 11, 1944.

23. To Richard, December 9, 1944.

24. To his wife, November 23, 1944.

25. To his wife, December 5, 1944.

26. To his wife, December 15, 1944.

27. Colonel Dolbey to the author, 1964.

28. To his parents, January 21, 1945.

29. To his wife, February 2, 1945.

30. In a letter to the author, March 6, 1965.

31. In a conversation with the author, October, 1966.

Chapter Four

1. To his father, October 9, 1944.

2. To his father, December 20, 1934.

3. To his wife, September 15, 1941.

4. To his parents, August 7, 1936.

5. In a conversation with the author, 1964.

6. In a letter to the author, 1967.

Chapter Five

1. Published by Longmans Green Ltd., 1927.

2. *R.E.,* p. 18.

3. To his father, January 27, 1935.

4. Oxford University Press, 1936.

5. To his father, January 4, 1935.
6. From "Journey to Oxford," typescript fragment.
7. *R.E.*, p. 2.
8. To his father, April 3, 1938.
9. The letter has been quoted in chap. 2, p. 40.
10. Henry Kerby to J. M., March 3, 1939.

Chapter Six

1. See Allen Curnow's poem "The Unhistoric Story" (in *A Small Room with Large Windows* [London, 1962], p. 7) where this phrase is the refrain.
2. *Man Alone* (second ed., Hamilton, N.Z., 1949), p. 110 (hereinafter abbreviated *M.A.*).
3. *Ibid.*, p. 21.
4. *Ibid.*
5. *Ibid.*
6. In his book *New Zealand 1826–7.*
7. Native villages.
8. *M.A.*, p. 9.

Chapter Seven

1. In his poem "The Unhistoric Story," see above, chap. 6, note 1.
2. To his wife, September 15, 1941.
3. *M.A.*, p. 17.
4. *Ibid.*
5. *Ibid.*, p. 18.
6. *Ibid.*, p. 19.
7. *Ibid.*
8. *Ibid.*, p. 20.
9. From *Imaginary Islands* (Auckland, 1950).
10. *M.A.*, p. 21.
11. *Ibid.*, p. 22.
12. *Ibid.*
13. *Ibid.*, p. 28.
14. *Ibid.*
15. *Ibid.*, p. 100.
16. *Ibid.*, p. 89.
17. *Ibid.*, p. 92.
18. *Ibid.*, p. 89.
19. *Ibid.*, p. 14.
20. *Ibid.*, p. 42.
21. *Ibid.*, p. 31.
22. *Ibid.*, p. 35.
23. *Ibid.*, p. 36.

24. *Ibid.*
25. *Ibid.*
26. *Ibid.*, p. 25.
27. *Ibid.*, p. 89.

Chapter Eight

1. "Rustic Witness," unpublished typescript.
2. *M.A.*, p. 189.
3. *Ibid.*, p. 37.
4. *Ibid.*, p. 156
5. Denis Glover, "The Magpies," from *Enter Without Knocking* (Christchurch, 1964).
6. *M.A.*, p. 75.
7. *Ibid.*, p. 136.
8. *Ibid.*, p. 142
9. *Ibid.*, p. 18.
10. *Ibid.*, p. 123.
11. *Ibid.*, p. 182.
12. *Ibid.*, p. 21.
13. E.g., Professor K. Sinclair in his *Penguin History of New Zealand.*
14. *M.A.*, p. 56.
15. *Ibid.*, p. 204.
16. *Ibid.*, p. 189.
17. *Ibid.*, p. 205.

Chapter Nine

1. *M.A.*, p. 207.
2. *R.E.*, p. 15.

Chapter Ten

1. Selected partly because it was the title of a poem by his former tutor, E. Blunden.
2. *R.E.*, p. 2.
3. *Ibid.*
4. *Ibid.*, p. 4.
5. *Ibid.*, p. 6.
6. *Ibid.*, p. 13.
7. *Ibid.*, p. 14.
8. *Ibid.*, p. 15.
9. *Ibid.*
10. *Ibid.*, p. 21.
11. *Ibid.*, p. 20.
12. *Ibid.*, p. 30.

Chapter Eleven

1. *R.E.*, p. 32.
2. *Ibid.*, p. 35.
3. *Ibid.*
4. *Ibid.*, p. 44.
5. *Ibid.*, p. 45.
6. *Ibid.*, p. 46.
7. *Ibid.*, p. 47.
8. *Ibid.*, p. 49.
9. *Ibid.*, p. 50.
10. *Ibid.*
11. *Ibid.*, original draft.
12. *Ibid.*, p. 64.
13. *Ibid.*, p. 66.
14. *Ibid.*, p. 68.
15. *Ibid.*, p. 77.
16. *Ibid.*, p. 78.
17. *Ibid.*, p. 80.
18. *Ibid.*, p. 94.
19. *Ibid.*, p. 116.
20. *Ibid.*, p. 121.
21. *Ibid.*, p. 125.
22. *Ibid.*, p. 137.
23. *Ibid.*, p. 139.
24. *Ibid.*, p. 145.

Chapter Twelve

1. *R.E.*, p. 149.
2. London, 1922.
3. *Disenchantment* (London, 1940), p. 186.
4. *Ibid.*, p. 240.

Selected Bibliography

(items are in chronological order)

PRIMARY SOURCES

"Sea Fever," a short story published under the pseudonym "Arnold Freydon" in *The Weekly Press*, Auckland, June 30, 1927.

Feature articles in *Auckland Star*, all signed "J.M."

"Summer in Oxford," July 14, 1934
"Children who Play," September 15, 1934 (an account of a visit to A. S. Neill's famous school)
"English Farming," (I), October 6, 1934
"English Farming," (II), October 13, 1934
"English Farming," (III), October 20, 1934
"English Farming," (IV), October 27, 1934
"English Farming," (V), November 3, 1934
"Life at Oxford," (I), December 1, 1934
"Life at Oxford," (II), December 8, 1934
"Life at Oxford," (III), December 15, 1934
"London Christmas," February 9, 1935
"Northern England," March 2, 1935
"East Anglia," May 25, 1935

"Behind the Cables" feature column in *Auckland Star* (written in collaboration with GEOFFREY S. COX) appeared on the following dates:

February 12, 1936	July 20, 1936
March 4, 1936	August 12, 1936
March 19, 1936	August 27, 1936
April 15, 1936	September 2, 1936
May 13, 1936	September 15, 1936
May 21, 1936	October 6, 1936
June 4, 1936	October 22, 1936
June 18, 1936	November 5, 1936
July 1, 1936	November 19, 1936

December 1, 1936   May 11, 1937
December 8, 1936   June 28, 1937
March 9, 1937

Poems of Freedom, ed. JOHN MULGAN (with an introduction by W. H.
AUDEN). London: Victor Gollancz, 1938.
The Concise Oxford Dictionary of English Literature, ed. JOHN MUL-
GAN. Oxford: Clarendon Press, 1939.
The Emigrants: Early Travellers to the Antipodes (in collaboration
with HECTOR BOLITHO). London: Selwyn and Blount, 1939.
Man Alone. London: Selwyn and Blount, 1939. Second Edition; Ham-
ilton, N.Z., Paul's, 1949. Reprinted 1960, 1965.
Report on Experience. London: Oxford University Press, 1947. Re-
printed Auckland, Paul's, 1967.
Introduction to English Literature (in collaboration with D. M. DAVIN).
Oxford: Clarendon Press, 1947.
Letters. Two large privately-held collections of Mulgan's letters have
been consulted. They are: (a) Those to his mother and father,
from 1933 till 1945. This is the property of Mr. R. G. MULGAN.
(b) Those to his wife from 1940 till 1945, which remain in the
possession of his widow, Mrs. GABRIELLE DAY.

SECONDARY SOURCES

BERTRAM, JAMES B. Review of *Man Alone* in *Tomorrow*, May 1, 1940.
An enthusiastic commendation of the book. Praises the dialogue—
"the most careful notation of common speech in these islands that
I have yet seen in print." Comments: "Here, at any rate, is one
novel that tells the truth about New Zealand."
REID, JOHN C. *Creative Writing in New Zealand*. Auckland: Whit-
combe and Tombs, 1946. Sees Johnson in *Man Alone* as "mod-
elled on Hemingway's 'dumb oxen' heroes." Accuses Mulgan of
lacking pity. This was one of the first published commentaries on
the novel. Brief, but perceptive, it pays tribute to the highlights
of the book—the riots, the Rangipo desert, etc.
HOLCROFT, M. H. Review of *Report on Experience* in *N.Z. Listener*,
August 13, 1947. Praises the New Zealand chapter. Notes how,
in the accounts of wartime action, Mulgan "remembers and judges
simultaneously." Calls the writing "clean and robust." Sums up
". . . may seem only a fragment; but there is in it a goodness and
truth and an artistic unity which may keep it alive when more ambitious books are forgotten."
HENRIQUES, ROBERT. Review of *Report on Experience* in *The Ob-*

server, October 19, 1947. By a coincidence, Mulgan's friend, G. S. Cox, has a book reviewed in the same notice—*Road to Trieste* (Heinemann, 1947). Henriques calls *Report on Experience* "a lovely document for a man to leave behind." He says it is written "with perception, poetry, and passion, and with a rare control. The reporter must have been a joyful, clear-sighted, modest man . . ."

ANON. Review of *Report on Experience* in the *Times Literary Supplement,* November 22, 1947. Rather an opaque review, which, perversely, considers Mulgan's account of the Greek guerrillas from the point of view of their military effectiveness, castigating them for inefficiency; and takes the book as though it were a manual for resistance fighters, of whom the reviewer disapproves. The chapters on England are applauded, however, as "the best character-study of a nation since Professor Brogan tried to explain the English to the Americans."

DAVIN, D. M. Review of *Report on Experience* in *Landfall,* II, 1 (March, 1948), 50–55 (reprinted as "John Mulgan" in *Landfall Country* [Christchurch, 1960]). The most farseeing comment on Mulgan yet published. The author detects the political interest which provided the chief stimulus for almost everything Mulgan did. Davin, a veteran of the New Zealand Division and a novelist himself, pays a warm and generous tribute to Mulgan's writing. He sees him as a type of "the man who remains true to his intellect . . . the martyr of our time."

BAXTER, JAMES K. Review of *Man Alone* in *Landfall,* III, 4 (December, 1949), 374–76. Seeking to interpret the book in terms of character drawing, Baxter finds it wanting. He recognizes the power of the novel, though uncertain of where the source of it is located.

McCORMICK, E. H. *New Zealand Literature: A Survey.* London: Oxford University Press, 1959. Notes, in *Man Alone,* the debt to Hemingway and the close reporting of the local scene, but space does not permit him to elaborate on these points. Of *Report on Experience* he gives a perceptive summary.

CAPE, PETER. Review of *Man Alone* (1960 reprint) in *N.Z. Listener,* March 17, 1961.

STEVENS, JOAN. *The New Zealand Novel 1860–1965* (Second Edition, revised to 1965). Wellington: A. H. & A. W. Reed, 1966. Professor Stevens repeats the myth that the title of *Man Alone* is a quotation from Hemingway. She appears to have thought that Part II is a carefully worked-in framework by which Part I is to be judged, but in a footnote allows that the way *Man Alone* was conceived and written should be taken into account. Useful questions about the technique of the novel are asked.

DAY, P. W. "Mulgan's *Man Alone*" in *Comment* (Wellington), VI, 4 (August, 1965), 15–22. Summarizes the biographical background of the writing of the novel, and attempts an interpretation in the light of this knowledge.

Index